TIMOTHY FINDLEY

From
Stone Orchard
A Collection of Memories

HarperFlamingoCanada

FROM STONE ORCHARD: A COLLECTION OF MEMORIES
Copyright © 1998 by Pebble Productions Inc.

http://www.harpercollins.com/canada

HarperCollins books may be purchased for educational, business, or sales promotional use. For information please write: Special Markets Department, HarperCollins Canada, 55 Avenue Road, Suite 2900, Toronto, Ontario M5R 3L2.

First edition

Canadian Cataloguing in Publication Data

Findley, Timothy, 1930–
From Stone Orchard : a collection of memories

Expanded versions of columns originally
published in Harrowsmith magazine.
ISBN 0-00-255729-0

1. Findley, Timothy — 1930– –Biography.   2. Farm life — Ontario —
Cannington Region — Biography.   3. Authors, Canadian (English) —
20th century — Biography.*   I. Title.

PS8511.I38Z53 1998   C813'.54   C98-931386-7
PR9199.3.F52Z468 1998

98 99 00 01 02 03 HC 10 9 8 7 6 5 4 3 2 1

Printed and bound in the United States

This book is dedicated to all who have shared the wonders of Stone Orchard: especially to Nelson Purvis and Leonard Griffin, who taught us how to live on a farm — and, above all, to Len Collins, who did so much to make it an unforgettable home.

To Stone Orchard

*W*HAT WE FOUND AND HOW WE FOUND IT, WHEN *Bill Whitehead and I went looking for a small farm near Toronto. It was 1964, just two years after we had both left the theatre and become writers. The curtain was about to go up on more than three decades of comedy, tragedy and romance.*

We found it because we had lost our way. It was the summer of 1964, and Bill Whitehead and I were looking for an affordable country property with an old house and the possibilities, we hoped, of a garden.

What we were seeking was not only a home, but a base for our new careers. After almost twenty years as an actor, I had just written my first novel. Bill, having worked both as research biologist and actor, was then moving into the world of writing documentaries in the arts and sciences — for radio, film and television. Toronto was our professional centre. That's where the work was. But since most of our writing could be done at home, what better workplace than an old farm? You can already see we were innocent romantics. And, looking back, I give thanks for that. Worldly sceptics must have the dullest lives on earth.

The trouble with new careers is they take time to produce an income. Hence, there was considerable emphasis on the *affordable* aspect of our search. By the time our weekend wanderings had finally brought us to a real-estate agent whose definition of affordability was even remotely close to ours, we were in a village never heard of by us. Very much heard of by its citizens. Cannington. *The Heart of Ontario.*

An old house on a small farm? our agent asked. *Well, there's one just down the road!* This way, we first set eyes on what was to become *Stone Orchard*.

What did we see? The gardens had gone wild. For five years, no one had lived here and the lawns were fields of hay. In the time before us, there had been a dairy farm here and all the buildings, fences and laneways had been devoted to the care and keeping of cattle and of those who tended them. There had not been much time for gardening, but a garden did exist — one huge rectangular bed that held a multitude of perennials: peonies, poppies, roses, irises and day lilies — all pushing forward to greet us, not unlike a welcoming committee.

There were lilac bushes, a few of which we were told were at least a hundred years old. And they were. Their trunks and branches were knotted ropes of bark and lichen. In the dooryard, there was an old wooden shed where the milk had been cooled in concrete basins full of water. Running between its roof and the roof of the house were cedar poles weighted down with grape vines. Between the front lawn and the road, a white wire fence stood in the shade of six gigantic maple trees — and, surrounding a small log hut that had once served as a root cellar, there was a grove of honey locusts — still the most beautiful trees we have.

Honeysuckle, chokecherries and apple trees gone wild made up most of the hedgerows, with giant elms, basswood trees and cedars standing above them. We were enchanted. I said then, and I still believe it: *we have come home.*

We were looking at a picture we now call "Before." "After," of course, came later. Then, what we saw was rustic, but full of promise. After twenty years or so, we came to live in the splendour of "After" — and it's hard to know which we have loved the most.

Although we have made many changes — expanding the

lawns, tearing down old fences and putting up new ones — the feeling is still the same as when we first arrived. Over time, we have taken the perennials we then encountered in oversized, undisciplined beds and redistributed them. They provide a sense of continuity that is vital to our love of Stone Orchard. They remind us of the pioneer hands that put them first in place. Even the ancient lilacs had to be moved to make room for an addition to the house. But they survived — thank heaven — and each spring their heavy, double blossoms still fill the air with their perfume — just as they did in the late 1800s.

Of course, our labours in the garden did not accomplish much at first. Cutting what lawn there was taught me I had muscles I had not ever put to work before — *scything muscles*: muscles in the middle back, muscles in the inner thighs, shoulder muscles that previous generations of men had taken for granted. For me, it was something of a nightmare.

On the other hand, nothing is so satisfying as lying down in a field you have cut yourself and staring up at the sky. I learned through this a whole new sense of respect for those who, coming from Europe, first cleared the fields of southern Ontario in the nineteenth century. All of the land in our community had once been covered with a forest of sugar maples. In the 1830s and '40s, most of the trees were felled by hand with saws and axes, the stumps dragged out of the earth by horses and oxen. And this was just the beginning.

We didn't call this place Stone Orchard for nothing. Stones are our principal crop! In the fence-rows, the giants are piled — ten to twelve feet in circumference — four to six feet thick. Some of these ancient monoliths were waiting for us as we dug our new foundations and ponds. Three of them now lie out in the open — monuments to the labours of our forebears. And then there are the others — the endless uprising of stones that every year's digging and ploughing pull to the surface.

I have set these out as border markers beside the paths and between the lawns and the flower-beds.

The house at Stone Orchard sits squarely in the middle of the east-west line. Fifty acres of land are spread out behind us. This means that a variety of locations has always been available for gardens — some in shade, others not; some behind gates, enclosed, and others open to the fields.

At first, it was enough to harvest the found fruit and vegetables that made up our early crops. A neighbour had ploughed up part of one field and planted potatoes there. He was happy to let us share them. In the same field, the previous owner had planted two long rows of asparagus. Innocent of any farming know-how, we asked our neighbour what was usually done with the asparagus in the fall. *Plough it under*, was the given advice — and that is what we did. We never saw the asparagus again, which was something of a botanical tragedy. It was more than twenty years before I succeeded in starting another asparagus bed and now, for two weeks each spring, we enjoy a small harvest. Bill prepares it as what we call a *Dutch Easter Breakfast* — served hot with hard-boiled eggs, also hot — slathered in melted butter and lemon juice.

We used the wild apples to make applesauce and cut them into our chili sauce as well. The wild grapes make excellent grape jelly that has something of an added "kick" to it, provided — we assume — by their wildness. For some years, we also made chokecherry jelly, but in the long run, given the fact that our professional workloads were growing, we had to give up most of the jellies and jams. This is one of the penalties, I guess, for increased assignments: you have to sacrifice some of the pleasures inherent in having your own produce — and your own time.

Spring, summer and autumn offered us a bounty of flowers — both from our oversized rectangle in the side yard and from

8

the fields. Again, it was all a question of becoming intimate with the land — and of learning to see more of what it had to offer. There's a hell of a lot more than dandelions and butter-cups out there! This you learn quite quickly. There are grasses, for instance, that we ultimately moved into our "formal" flower-beds — grasses that make wonderful "fernery" for jars, along with daisies, star flowers, purple vetch and Queen Anne's lace. Add a few day lilies and you could enter the arrangements in the local flower show. I've never done this, but only because I'm too shy. The other entrants would wipe my modest efforts off the map. Nonetheless, setting out the treasures of the wild in an ironstone pitcher or a small blue glass remains one of my greatest pleasures.

Thirty-two years — and many mementos. All the animal graves. Our parents' ashes and my brother's. Six dogs, two-by-two, walked over every inch of ground, through the fields and into the woods. All the people who have loved it here as much as we do. The riotous mayhem wrought by dozens of guests and one small bathroom; the night the bed fell (*pace* James Thurber), exposing the occupants, who were making love, to the shouts and screams of the rest of us who were *not* making love; and the dinner party when everyone went outside in the twilight, dressed like royalty, napkins and wine glasses in hand, to watch a herd of deer, with a majestic stag, pass through the gardens, pausing to eat our grass.

Yes. And the reminders of those who worked here. A dip in the lawn that was turned into a perfect lily pond with a Buddha and a Japanese stone lantern. Jimmy Roots's stone steps and path. All the wonders built by Len Collins — including the palatial martin house — and his greatest gift: his enduring friendship. Len and Anne and their three incredible children — Maureen, Caileigh and Brandon — have become a vital part of our own family.

We are lucky — privileged. Yes, we created it and yes, it nearly killed us at times. But what Stone Orchard has given back, to us and to others, is beyond calculation. We had no idea what we were doing. It was — and it remains — a gift.

Most of what follows was written as a series of columns published in the bi-monthly magazine *Harrowsmith*, starting in 1993. Two of the pieces are new: *Literary Landmarks* and *The Kitchen Stove*. Parts of this introduction first appeared under the title *When This You See* in the magazine *Toronto Life Gardens*. The original *Harrowsmith* pieces, written to fit on a single page, have here been expanded to include additional anecdotes and, occasionally, to reflect the fact that passing years bring both arrivals and departures.

Now, time has brought the moment for me and Bill to leave this haven. The loss of it can never be accommodated. Nothing replaces loss. Nothing. Does one life compensate another? Never. Still, we have what we had — and what we have. The pond in all its summer glory and with its winter skaters shooting pucks across the ice; the woods in their dense green light beyond the moss-encrusted fences; the dogs I walked through fields of corn and hay and the cats at every turn. All the people whose figures haunt the landscape there. And all the vistas spreading out on every side. *Unforgettable — unforgotten.*

Aging, Bill and I will work until we drop, but we can no longer afford the time and energy that Stone Orchard's wonders demand. We are grateful beyond words for the adventure and the privilege of being in that magic place — and of being a part of the Cannington community. Our years there have provided us with far, far more than memories. They have given us the spirit on which survival depends.

Living with the Past

*S*TONE ORCHARD'S FIRST OWNER ARRIVED 125 YEARS *before we did. The past, we found, was still there — in the house and in its property, in the community at large and throughout the surrounding countryside.*

Looking Back

When Bill and I moved into Stone Orchard that summer of 1964, we arrived too late to plant a garden. Nelson Purvis, the former owner whose parents had lived here, still farmed next door.

"There's six rows of potatoes in your northwest field," he told us. "If you fellows want to dig them, help yourself." We lived one whole week on those potatoes, augmented by a pound of bacon and some puffballs we found in the lane. The lowly spud is oft neglected, and it shouldn't be. Mashed with green onions, baked with butter, diced in a salad, steamed, boiled, fried or scalloped — the variations are endless. But we soon discovered the northwest field was going to yield us more than delicious tubers.

The very first forkful of earth contained the blue-and-white spout of an old teapot. Shards of sepia-coloured pottery followed and, over the next days, aged gin jars, cracked grey stoneware and an alarming number of nineteenth-century medicine bottles. Perhaps the place had once been occupied by raving dipsomaniacs and pale, languid invalids of the kind described in Victorian novels. But what disease or illness could possibly require so much medication?

By this time we had come to know Nelson Purvis not only as a generous neighbour, but also as a diviner, a ragtime piano player and a man who enjoyed cigarettes that were rolled by hand in newsprint. To say the least, he was interesting. One day, Nels came by and looked at our growing collection of artifacts in the kitchen. As he fingered the various objects we had found, enigmatically deadpan, he said, "You fellows believe in the transmigration of souls?"

Well — no. Not then. But this, I think, was Nelson's way of telling us what we were finding was more than mere shards. In a manner that can only be described as *presence*, we had already felt a sense of occupation in the house. Nothing visual. Nothing audible. Simply an awareness — quite pacific — that someone had left behind a palpable infusion of character — and of contentment.

Nelson had given us a complete set of deeds, reaching all the way back to 1839, when the property, then twice its present fifty acres, was sold by the Canada Company to a man called MacMillan — for the sum of fifty pounds. Ultimately, a family named MacLean ran a dairy farm here after the First World War. This explained all those old milk bottles under the floor of the drive-shed, but the medicine bottles remained a mystery.

One day, when I was walking the dogs in the lower meadow, I paused near a corner where the snake-rail fence met a pile of boulders dragged there from the fields. Rather quickly, I was overwhelmed by a strong sense of the people who had lived here during the time this fence was built. I could see them in my mind, quite whole — the way one might remember a photograph. A short, sharp-featured man in shirt and trousers paused from his labours to receive a honey pail of water brought from the house by a woman in a nineteenth-century grey dress. I'm not talking about ghosts here. I'm

suggesting an aura — benign, contented, creative and generous. But who had lent their presence to this atmosphere?

Enter Islay Lambert, a columnist for the *Cannington
Gleaner*, our community newspaper. Week by week, Islay had
been writing a local history as her Centennial project. When
she saw our deeds, she pointed to the one dated 1848. *Alfred
Wyatt,* it read. Young Mister Wyatt had come out from
Britain as a pharmacist, she told us. "He set up his shop in
what is now your dining-room."

At last, we had an explanation for all those medicine
phials and bottles. Not the explanation we had expected; I
had been so concerned about that imaginary invalid. And
when it came time to renovate the dining-room, replacing
its brittle plasterboard with new drywall, we discovered a
nineteenth-century pharmaceutical catalogue nestled in
behind one of the baseboards, just where it must have fallen
— one day, long ago.

The young man who undertook our renovations at Stone
Orchard figures largely in our part of its history. This was —
and is — our neighbour Len Collins. Starting in 1979, Len
worked with us for more than ten years, day in, day out.
Then, married and a father, he needed to take on more work
than could afford to offer him. In recent years, therefore,
he's been with us part-time only, but during his full-time years
he built, single-handed, the final extension to the house, kept
us sane during blizzards, flood and power failures (by solving
all the attendant problems); planted and tended the vegetable
gardens, mended fences, fed the dogs and cats in our extended
absences and oversaw our safety.

Stripping away the plaster in the dining-room, Len discovered the old pine planks that made up part of the walls' original structure. They were an inch thick, up to eighteen inches
wide — utterly beautiful and pristine. *It would be a shame*

just to cover these up with drywall, he told us. *All right,* we countered, *do something with them.*

That "something" turned out to be a pair of built-in, glass-shelved china cupboards, their wood a perfect match to the nineteenth-century Ontario pine dining-room suite we had acquired a few years before. Thus, we were able to display some of our family heirlooms — along with a few of Alfred Wyatt's unearthed medicine bottles, in a setting that bespoke their own time.

I wondered what Alfred Wyatt might have looked like. And his wife, whose name, we learned, was Charlotte. Charlotte Thompson's father, a major in the British army, once lived just down the road from us. *Major* Thompson? That's when we discovered this area had been settled by retired military officers, most of them veterans of the Napoleonic Wars. They were kept on half pay for some years if they agreed to take up residence in the New World. While the officers chose land near us, the men were sent about ten miles farther north to the shores of Lake Simcoe, around what is now the town of Beaverton. This, too, explained a previously mystifying factor — the rivalry between our two communities.

Bill and I had become magnets for facts and artifacts that revealed our local history. But still, I wondered, could the Wyatts have been the figures I imagined down in the field by the fence?

In Centennial Year, all the stores in Cannington put forth displays of mementos of the town's past. One of the two drugstores then was run by old Mister Henderson. Even in his nineties, he still opened up his store every day. Nonetheless, Mister Henderson refused to offer some of his stock for sale. Certainly, he could not be made to part with any of the dusty old thirties' scribblers I coveted — or the bottles of ink or the wooden pens with brass nibs. Still, he enjoyed the company of anyone who ventured inside — and one day that was me.

I should note here that after Mister Henderson's death, his daughter, Edna Eastman, very kindly saw to it that I fell heir to a few of those priceless scribblers and pens.

Back in 1967, Mister Henderson's shop window displayed a photograph that had caught my attention. It showed a young man standing beside a figure who seemed somehow to be known to me. He was short and sharp-featured and even though he was white-haired and greatly old, he gazed from the photograph in a familiar fashion. It was our pharmacist, Alfie Wyatt, seen near the end of his life. And standing beside him was Mister Henderson in his youth: a living link with the past. One handshake carried me back to the 1840s, and to the days when Alfie Wyatt built his fences, pausing only long enough to drink the fresh, cold water from Charlotte's honey pail.

Now, every time I walk or ride my bicycle up the hill to the west of us, I wave at the little cemetery there and call out "good morning, Alfie!" and to Charlotte, "good morning!" And I thank them — not only for building the house where we live, but for infusing it with so much spirit.

Wildwood

There is always snow before Christmas — dusting the landscape, turning the ploughed fields into sepia photographs and the pioneer fences into black-and-white drawings. Most of the fences at Stone Orchard were constructed at least a century ago of rails that were split from cedars grown in our own woodlot.

The woodlot itself is hemmed on three sides with these fences and by a marshy tract of willow scrub on the other. It stands, not unlike a separate kingdom, at the foot of a hill and I often go down there — just to be there; no other reason. There is a second stand of trees nearby, not yet mature enough for cutting. The cattle have established wallows in open spaces among the trees, where their summer lyings and tramplings have done away with any hope of undergrowth. In the larger, older woodlot, the undergrowth is lush and varied: ferns where there is least light; wildflowers, shrubs and young trees on the verges. The light itself is moss-green — filtered and filigreed, broken from time to time by sudden shafts of sunlight as the wind blows holes twenty feet up in the canopy of cedar fronds.

I cannot tell how old the woodlot is, though I know from reading Catherine Parr Traill, it was more than likely an afterthought. In her book *The Backwoods of Canada*, published in

1836, Traill describes the clearing of the land north of Lake Ontario with fire. This was still the preferred method in the mid-1840s, when the area around Stone Orchard was opened up to British settlers. We are on a parallel and only forty-odd miles to the east of where Mrs Traill and her husband, Tom, homesteaded near Lakefield, Ontario. The fires would sometimes "continue unextinguished for days," she tells us. Afterward, the ashes were spread to fertilize the stump-dotted fields. Sometimes the burnings got out of control and flared out into the surrounding forests, causing havoc and further waste. It was only after these accidental fires had begun to take their toll that the settlers realized they were in danger of stranding themselves in a world without trees. And thus, the institution of the woodlot — as a source of both firewood and fencing.

By the time we had finished renovating and enlarging the original house at Stone Orchard, we ended up with two fireplaces and two wood-burning stoves. Firewood was therefore an important item on our list of essentials — and we had a variety of ways of acquiring it.

In addition to what we got from the woodlot, there was always a dead tree or a series of dead branches to be dealt with. Mostly, these trees were the victims of Dutch Elm disease. Since neither of us is adept at handling a chain saw, it was usually Len Collins or one of the teenagers who converted the deadwood to firewood. At first, this was piled up beside the driveway — neatly, if time allowed; helter-skelter, if Bill and I were on the run with our writing.

The woodpile was inevitably popular with a variety of animal life. Snakes, spiders — the occasional salamander, if the rains were extra heavy — and once, what we at first took to be a pair of rabbits. We would catch only a glimpse of them — small brown critters — disappearing into the darker recesses of the pile. Eventually, we discovered they were, in fact, a pair of kittens — two of the many such abandoned pets who were simply dumped at our gate by strangers. We finally persuaded them to trust us, and added them to our expanding feline population. Neither ever grew very large, which was reflected in the name of the smallest one — Childie — while with the other, we commemorated the site of their first home on the property — Woodie.

At first, when we put down bowls of food, the "rabbit cats" would not come out to eat unless we stood at least ten paces off. Then one day, Woodie came to the house, which she had never done before, and seemed to be in distress. No sooner had I gone outside than she started away towards the woodpile. Clearly, I was to follow. Once we reached the woodpile, Woodie tried to dig down through the logs. Taking her example, I pulled away a layer or two until I came to a nest of grass and straw where Childie lay. She was shivering and her eyes were glued shut with dried rheum. She was very nearly dead. I brought them both inside the house, where they stayed in the warmth until Childie recovered. This way, we learned that woodpiles yield more than wood.

Our greatest single source of firewood came when we had to take down the mighty "milking tree" — a huge old elm that had become diseased. It got its name before our time, when the cattle were milked in its shade. The hydro crew did the cutting and dismantling, since theirs was the only equipment large enough to handle the massive trunk and limbs. To everyone's amazement, when the tree was finally felled, we discovered a young raccoon, huddled in an opening that had been so high on the trunk, we had never noticed it. I will not soon forget the expression on that raccoon's face as we peered into its nest. Fear . . . resignation . . . and a bid for pity. Needless to say, we suspended the operation until the animal left of its own accord, sometime in the night. It may well have been the ancestor of the generations of raccoons who have lived in the loft of our unused barn for many years, and whose offspring join the cats most spring nights for a snack of kibble on the back porch.

The fireplace in the living-room is the major consumer of our wood — and as we sit there in front of it, we often find that it wins out over the television in the competition for our attention. Perhaps it's because an open fire recalls the generations who depended on it for all their heating and cooking — and to some degree for their safety. Or perhaps it is simply an inherent fascination with the beauty of flames and the pictures they weave. Whatever the reason, we've never regretted our decision to install the fireplaces and the wood stoves.

These days, most of our kindling and some new fenceposts are still drawn from the woodlot down at the foot of the hill. The other stand of trees is left to the cattle — not our cattle, but those belonging to whichever neighbour is using our land as pasture. I spend some time down there in every season, but not at the height of summer, when blackflies, mosquitoes and horseflies crowd the air. The moment I set foot beyond the first ring of trees, the insect buzzword for human blood spreads like one of Mrs Traill's fires. In the fall and winter, however, I can stand at the centre by the great fallen tree whose uprooted trunk is a landmark there and pass whole hours while the dogs range out in search of rabbit smells and skunk trails.

The deer, foxes and brush wolves have created paths that I use to enter or to leave the wood at its southern reaches. These trails are useful to the dogs but can be treacherous to an upright human being, since they are made by beasts whose shape and stature have little or nothing in common with mine. The hooves and shanks of a deer, for instance, have ways of dealing with roots and brush that my feet and shins cannot manage. Animal necks are better, too, at dipping through the lower branches of the trees than my short neck and waving arms.

Still, I go there — pushing along these paths, or clambering over the fences to seek the stillness that only a woods can provide. I am in awe of it and never fail to find a kind of peace at the centre that I can carry home up the hill. I am the container in which that peace is carried. Looking back from the crest, I will often see a flight of birds go up that I had failed to see when standing near them — or a porcupine swaying in the branches of the tallest tree, asleep in a cradle I will never know. His dreaming there, however, has something in common, I am certain, with my own. We both go down to the woods to find some safety — he from the dogs at his feet and me from the wind at the top of the hill.

The Writing in the Wall

Some years ago, we made a final addition to the house. At the second-storey level, this meant cutting through what had been an outside wall in order to put in a connecting doorway. Len Collins, who was building the new wing practically single-handed, set about stripping off the 1848 siding. Midstrip, so to speak, he called to Bill and me to come and see what he'd found. One of the exposed planks bore the nineteenth-century pencilled jottings of the carpenter who had built the original house. This was a series of annotated calculations just like the ones we had seen Len scribble a hundred times onto scraps of wood as he figured out the next cut of the saw — the next angle of stress — the next place-ment in a pattern. The 1840s' pencilled notes were oddly compelling — poignant and moving. I could see the man himself, bending to his present task, squinting at his fractions on a sunny day, whistling, as Len does, while he calculates the making of the house we live in.

That was not the first time we'd read the writings in and on our walls. In the 1960s, we tore down the original drive-shed in order to build a new one. Pinned to the timbers in behind some boards was an ancient parcel done up in oiled paper and tied with binder twine. Once we'd unwrapped it and carefully unfolded the brittle sheets of paper inside, we were able to read the news of the first days of the Boer War as reported in the Toronto *Evening Star* on a mid-October day in 1899. Accompanying this relic was a note, written with elegant Victorian penmanship. It told of that day's weather ("sunny, with a bit of haze") and of the view from the shed's upper storey ("the Ellis School at the corner . . . and the river down the hill to the west"). It bore a signature that, unlike the rest of the note, was unreadable. "Me," it might have said. "Me" or "I" — but nothing else decipherable. This too was oddly compelling, poignant and moving.

Our unexplained and unexpected find inevitably called to mind what once had been seen here — in the days of the first British settlers — all the way back to the time before the land was cleared, squared off and latticed with roads and hydro lines — the time when what stretched from horizon to horizon was a sea of trees.

A vivid reminder of those times still lives on the Georgina Islands in nearby Lake Simcoe — the descendants of the Ojibway hunters of the past. My father, born in 1902, remembered Granny Big Canoe's stories, as she sat having tea with the Findley family in the kitchen of their summer cottage at Jackson's Point. And when Bill and I worked as actors at the Red Barn Theatre on Simcoe's south shore, Lorenzo Big Canoe was chief of the resident band. Hand over hand, we touch one another generation by generation. Time is briefer than we think.

Nelson Purvis, who sold us Stone Orchard, told of his own discoveries from those forested times, turned up year after year by the ploughing of his fields. Animal bones and broken knives, arrowheads and pottery shards that spoke of temporary native encampments. One such area lies on a ridge running along the top of the field behind our barn. Another borders the Beaver River, just south of the bridge down the road. As a boy, Nelson learned that the Lake Simcoe bands used our local waterways whenever they needed to venture into the hunting grounds of the Kawartha Lakes to the east. (*Kawartha*, by the way, is not a native name, but the invention of an early Peterborough Chamber of Commerce member, eager to bolster the tourist trade!)

Nelson's archaeological findings are what I call *writing on the walls of time* — vivid in their articulation of human activity as any pencilled annotation. *We passed this way — we paused — went on — and returned.*

The walls of this house have witnessed almost all of my own activity as a writer. Except for a few early stories and the first two novels, all my books have been begun — and most of them have been completed — on the property we call Stone Orchard. I've written upstairs and downstairs, on the front porch, in the kitchen, under a trellised hop vine out behind the log cabin that once served as a root cellar — and, most recently, in the gazebo beside the pond. I have yet to write on the walls. Perhaps I will, in time.

On the other hand, my writings were once spread across an entire wall of my study. I was starting a novel that, oddly enough, included several kinds of "writing on the wall." It was called *Famous Last Words*, and it dealt with the rise of Fascism before World War II. In the book's final form, much of the story was inscribed by the leading character on the walls of an abandoned hotel in the Austrian Alps. Before I had encountered either the character or the walls upon which he wrote, I had thought I was writing a book about a power play within the Canadian establishment, and for the first time, I decided to scheme out the whole book before starting to write.

There were more than thirty leading characters — and so I

laboriously wrote out thirty sets of filing cards, detailing their life histories, their roles in the novel, their relationship with other characters — and so on. I then pinned the cards to my study wall — and began to "compose." Hah! It was a disaster.

By the time I was through, the story had changed so much that only two of the cards were still in place. The rest had all been taken down and burned. I have never since attempted to pre-plot a novel. For me, the proverbial "writing on the wall" was simplicity itself. And it said: *just sit down and write.*

The more we both wrote — Bill and I — the more we were able to extend our contributions to Stone Orchard. In the early 1970s, we built a fieldstone wall across the front of the property. Just as it was nearly finished, we remembered what we had found in the original drive-shed and I decided we too must leave a time capsule — a message for some future reader, telling of our own era and culture. The stonemason was willing to place something under the last stone — but it had to be done right away. The "mud," as he called the mortar, would soon be too hard to work with. I hurried into the house. What better symbols of our time than a Coke bottle and some coins? I grabbed a piece of paper and wrote something appropriate about who we were and what role these artifacts had played in our society — dated it, rolled it up and thrust it into the Coke bottle. Next, I forked out a handful of coins from my pocket. Drat! They were too big for the narrow mouth of the receptacle. The mason was shouting: *get a move on!* In the pantry, I grabbed an empty mayonnaise jar — broke the Coke bottle in the sink, retrieved the note — thrust it into the jar — rained my coins in on top and ran out to the mason. He laid the time capsule in place, slapped on the remains of his "mud" and worked the final stone into position. Done! It was a thrilling moment.

That night, I had a terrible thought. In my haste, I had forgotten to change the note. Now, I am haunted by the image of some future archaeologist, finding a mortar-encrusted jar in the ruins of an ancient stone wall and claiming her place in history as the discoverer of a hitherto unknown society from the distant twentieth century: *The Wide-Mouthed Coke-Jar Culture of Cannington, Ontario*. Blessings on her. I hope she will forgive me once the faded letters on its lid have been deciphered. *H-l-m-n- M-y-n-a-s-*. Sorry.

Literary Landscapes

It was not long after moving into the house at Stone Orchard that we discovered with amazement just how apt our choice of property had been — given that we both were making our living as writers. A look at the mailboxes along our road — plus a few conversations in the village — revealed that among our neighbours were none other than James and Nora Joyce, Karl Marx, Billy Budd and Mister C. Isherwood.

This seemed to be a good omen, and we were also pleased to find that close by there were other literary locations of great interest.

The village of Leaskdale lay about twelve miles to the southwest, on our chosen route to Toronto. We first became aware of its claim to fame when, in 1967, an historical plaque was erected on Highway 12, showing tourists the way to the Ontario home of L. M. Montgomery, creator of *Anne of Green Gables*. The author was married to a Presbyterian minister, and Leaskdale was the centre of her husband's parish. When the historical plaque was first installed, it bore the astounding revelation that those famous initials, L. M., stood for *Ludy Maud*. "Ludy Maud! Ludy Maud!" It had the look and the ring of the heroine's name in a southern gothic novel. And so it was with both interest and disappointment that we later discovered the original plaque had been replaced by another that read, correctly: *Lucy Maud Montgomery*. Still, whenever we drive past the white stuccoed house that once had been hers, we call out *Good day, Ludy Maud!*

For the first few times, on our early-morning drives through Leaskdale, it came as a surprise to discover busloads of Japanese tourists taking photographs of the Montgomery house. This was before we learned how enduringly popular the Green Gables books are in Japan, where Lucy Maud Montgomery is their best-loved Canadian writer. I am happy to say that two Findley novels have been translated into Japanese, but — so far — no busloads of tourists have stopped in front of Stone Orchard.

We already knew of a nearby location linked to another popular writer: Mazo de la Roche — world famous for her Jalna books. She is buried in the graveyard of a lovely little Anglican church on the south shore of Lake Simcoe, near the entrance to Sibbald Provincial Park — about twenty-five kilometres from our farm. I've often wondered — was she really Maisie Roach? She certainly had roots in that region, which features an area known as Roach's Point. Some of my own roots lie not far away; my Grandfather Findley grew up in the nearby town of Sutton — then known as Sutton West. Barely more than a stone's throw from Mazo's grave is the handsome Edwardian cottage that was once my grandfather's summer home at Jackson's Point. These twin communities are now perhaps best known as the home of Peter Gzowski. The literary connection persists.

Long ago — so it seems — in the summer of 1962, Bill and I had lived in a tiny cabin that lies between the graveyard and the old Findley cottage. Tiny? Yes — before our occupation of it, it had been a roadside Coca-Cola stand. Still, it had room for two cots, two chairs and a bureau. Given that we were both spending most of our time rehearsing and performing at Jackson's Point's Red Barn Theatre, it was quite adequate. On looking back, however, I don't know why we didn't augment our incomes by selling Coke and Pepsi in our off-hours.

Right beside the Red Barn is the popular resort known as The Briars. It was once the country mansion of the Sibbald family, one of whose descendants, John, is still involved with both the resort and the theatre. It has long been my private belief that the beautiful old house and its original outbuildings — including a peacock house — were the inspiration for Mazo's Jalna, the home of the fictional Whiteoaks. Given her descriptions of the geography in those books, I see no reason why the lake in her stories has to be Lake Ontario and not Lake Simcoe. The Sibbalds originally came to Canada from an imperial British outpost in India, and they too were headed by a matriarch — just like the Whiteoaks family. I suppose it's neither here nor there, but the similarities continue to intrigue me.

The Anglican graveyard at Jackson's Point holds the remains of yet another renowned literary figure — Stephen Leacock. We were once given a gift by Peter Sibbald Brown — a publisher and artist who lives nearby — which was evidence of just how renowned Leacock must indeed have been. It is now framed and in my study: an envelope addressed — and delivered — to *Stephen Leacock, Canada*.

Bill and I often visit that lakeshore cemetery. Its church — a small but beautiful stone building — houses stained-glass windows designed by the daughters of Governor Simcoe in the early nineteenth century, and it was there that one of our former teenage helpers was married.

To the east of Cannington — about forty miles away — is the area homesteaded by the famous Strickland sisters,

Catharine Parr Traill and Susanna Moodie, who came to Canada from Britain in the 1830s. Mrs Moodie, of course, is the author of that classic of pioneer life in Ontario, *Roughing It in the Bush*. The site of her home — and of her sister's — are near Lakefield, north of Peterborough. For most of our time at Stone Orchard, Lakefield was the home of a more recent writer, the late Margaret Laurence.

Margaret was an old friend whose visits to our farm we always enjoyed. There was never a lack of fun and laughter with Margaret around. One visit was particularly memorable — and for a moment, almost aborted.

This is what had happened. We had told another friend, the naturalist, John Livingston, why we had jokingly given our swimming pool a special name. It had to do with the fact that Bill's Great-Uncle George had, as a young lawyer, shared offices in Calgary with R. B. Bennett, a former Canadian prime minister. When George was emasculated by shrapnel in World War I, he returned home and — as Bill tells it — being of good prairie practicality, he married a woman who moved her lesbian companion into the household. It was apparently a happy arrangement all round. Bill knew the companion as Great Aunt Ted. In the fullness of time, R. B. Bennett died and left a small legacy to his old friend George. The money then passed first to his wife and then, on her death, to Great-Aunt Ted who, having no other family, decided to divide it amongst some of her friend's nieces — including Bill's mother. Next thing we knew, the money had been passed on to us as a gift to help set up our new home. There was just enough for a swimming pool — which, of course, we referred to as the R. B. Bennett Memorial Pool.

And so . . . John Livingston came to the farm one day when we were away, and installed a professionally painted sign beside the pool, declaring its name for all the world to see. We were in Lakefield collecting Margaret Laurence. When we got home, and when Margaret saw the name of Bennett — whom she and many westerners blamed for the Great Depression — she was ready to be driven straight back to Lakefield. Once we had explained, however, she roared with laughter and agreed to stay. No swimming in the Bennett pool, but otherwise a happy time.

A final word about those famous literary names to be found in our immediate landscape. Nora Joyce, who lives down the road, became our housekeeper — while her son, James, is now a dentist west of Toronto. Karl Marx — spelled, in Cannington, Carl Mark — ran our local gas station until his death a few years ago. Billy Budd was the son of a neighbour, and as a cherubic blond teenager, sold us horse manure for the garden. Now, he travels as a harness-racing driver. As for Mister C. Isherwood — sadly, before we could meet him, he moved away from the little house at the corner. Pity. I've often wondered if Sally Bowles ever came to visit him there.

Going . . . Going . . .

"Six pressed-back maple chairs in mint condition: what am I bid? Shall we start at a dollar apiece! One dollar! No?"

As I put my hand in the air, the auctioneer continued: "Well, then — seventy-five. Come on, folks, seventy-five cents each. *Yes.* I have seventy-five!" He had finally seen my waving hand. "Do I hear one dollar?"

No, he did not hear one dollar. Extraordinarily enough, that day in the nearby village of Vallentyne, nobody else was interested in pressed-back chairs. And so they sat around our kitchen table from 1965 until, more than twenty years later, the building of a breakfast nook caused them to be shifted to an honourable place on the screened-in porch, where we often eat lunch. Honourable — and respected. When friends recently managed to bid successfully on similar chairs, the price was more than a hundred dollars each.

We have attended scores of these auctions over the years — where the leftovers of family life are set out on the lawn of a house emptied by death, old age or relocation. The sale in Vallentyne was memorable — not only for how much we came to love the chairs, or for their shamingly low cost — but for the fact, as we later discovered, that Bill's great-grandfather had been an innkeeper just a few hundred feet from the old manse from which the chairs were sold. Perhaps he had once occupied one, sitting with the minister, taking tea — or some other beverage more in his own line.

A second memorable auction is one I'd rather forget. It was in a town north of Toronto, just before we moved to Stone Orchard. Among its listed items was an upright piano. My maternal grandfather had run a piano factory in the early years of the century; my parents met as my father was playing the piano at a party; and though I never did learn to read music, I loved to play — by ear. And so we bid on the piano — and were eventually outbid, and saddened. However, a woman standing near us said that *she* had an upright piano, if we'd like to follow her home and inspect it. This we did. And when I sat down and began to play, the mellowness of both its voice and of the old-gold oak of its construction was truly exciting. "We've *got* to have it!" I exclaimed to Bill. "I don't care *what* it costs!"

Now, as Bill tells the story, he then had to sit down and negotiate an affordable price with my determined words ringing in the air. Expensive? Yes — but worth every penny. I played its keys for more than thirty years and, when the time came, alas, to leave Stone Orchard, the piano was moved across the road, where it is now enjoyed by three Collins children and by Anne, their mother. One of the things I learned from the stories my mother so often told of her father's piano factory is that *every piano has its own voice*. And the voice of my own piano still sings in my ears.

Many of Stone Orchard's rooms have been furnished and decorated — in part, anyway — from rural auctions. A brass bed . . . a pair of maple bureaus . . . a pie-crust table . . . the splendid kerosene chandelier that hangs in the dining-room, complete with gleaming red glass shade and pendants. This latter, bought in Lumsden, Saskatchewan, went for more than seventy-five cents, but time has erased the exact amount from memory. What is most vividly remembered is the journey by car from Lumsden to Cannington, during which the lamp, with all its crystals wrapped in Facelle tissues, rode in blanketed splendour, surrounded by cautionary layers of clothing on the back seat. On that journey, we might as well have been chauffeurs to royalty! But we got it home safely and now it hangs in the dining-room of our house in France, having hung for all those years in the dining-room at what I still call "home": Stone Orchard.

I've often wondered why more young people starting out to furnish a house or apartment don't head for the country and see what's available. It's true, something that can be resold as an antique may fetch a lot of money, but there are still sturdy and attractive pieces of furniture from the twenties and thirties that cost a lot less — and last a lot longer — than anything made more recently.

Besides, just to *be* at one of these auctions is an experience worth having. If there's a large and shifting crowd, you can have the amusing but also infuriating problem — as Bill and I have done — of unintentionally bidding against your own partner. Or you can be lucky enough to end up with an unexpected treasure.

Len Collins, Sr. and his wife, Jewell, were at a local auction recently, when Jewell spotted an old gilt frame in almost mint condition. She bid, and kept bidding. Eventually, she got it. When she arrived home, Jewell decided to discard the rather faded floral print the frame contained. But! On removing it, Jewell discovered some writing on the back, and a date: 1862. Thinking, *Tiff is interested in old things*, she sent the print over to us, and proceeded to choose whatever she would put in its place.

Well. And I mean, WELL. . . .

We read what was written there in the elegant, spidery hand that was common to the mid-nineteenth century. What we read was a poem entitled "Britannia's Wreath." Each of its four stanzas dealt with the symbols of what was only then beginning to be known as the United Kingdom: the rose, the thistle, the shamrock and the leek. The poem was not only dated, it was signed. *S. Moodie, Belleville.*

Of course, we knew that Susanna Moodie had lived in Belleville, Ontario, in her later years — but, still. . . . Could it possibly be? Just to be sure, we spoke to a friend at Trent University, in nearby Peterborough — Michael Peterman, who happens to be a Moodie scholar. Would he like to come to lunch, and put us out of our misery? He would. And he brought with him a bundle of Moodie letters he had recently unearthed.

There was no need, however, even to refer to them. As soon as Michael looked at the back of the print, he nodded. *Yes*, it was a Moodie poem — one she had written before coming to Canada — and *yes*, it was in her own hand. Then he turned the print over. And *yes*, she had painted the picture.

Painted the picture? *Yes*, again. It was not a print. It was an example of the gifts Susanna and her daughters used to present to their friends — watercolours or drawings of flowers.

Well, what else could we do. Happily, we presented Jewell's trophy — with her blessing — to Michael Peterman.

A very few years later, Susanna Moodie became a character in one of my novels — *Headhunter.* As well as pioneer, writer and artist, Moodie was also an avid spiritualist. This, in itself, suited my needs. Plus the fact that Susanna took an interest, in its early days, in Toronto's new Asylum for the Insane. This, too, fitted perfectly into the storyline of the book. What, I wonder, would Susanna Moodie make of the fact that all the years she endured the rigours of the backwoods and all the years she devoted to bringing that struggle to life in words have become the stuff of novels and plays and poems by the likes of Margaret Atwood, Carol Shields, Tom King and T.F.?

Quite apart from the adventure of unheralded discoveries, auctions are truly magnetic. There is something both moving and intriguing about the display of symbols that represent whole lifetimes — often the collected wonders of several generations. Furniture that's been handed down from great-great-grandparents; photographs of unnamed relatives, abandoned in gilt frames — some of which we've rescued and hung on our own walls; books with faded nineteenth-century marginalia; incomplete sets of practically anything — dishes, flatware, tools, games and sports equipment. All the things people can't quite bring themselves to give or throw away. Going . . . going . . . but not forgotten. Never forgotten if they find new homes and lives.

I will never forget watching one elderly woman — the epitome of the phrase *little old lady* — as she made her way about a Cannington auction. As I saw her moving slowly along the rows of boxes, it was all too easy to understand that what she regarded was the household wares — the dishes, glasses, cutlery and objects of one of her recently deceased contemporaries. Suddenly, she stopped, and picked up a blue cup and saucer. The image was unavoidable — two friends sharing tea and gossip through the years. We weren't the only ones who had noticed her. When the auctioneer reached that lot number, and asked for a starting bid of twenty-five cents — only one aged hand was raised. Somehow, the word had spread, and everyone else stood aside and smiled as the little old lady claimed her prize and walked away. *Going . . . going . . . going . . . but not gone.*

Field Work

*F*ARMS AND GARDENS ARE DESIGNED FOR GROWTH, *but what they yield may include a growing sense of contentment — and the occasional surprise.*

Sanctuary

There is an enclosure at Stone Orchard which was once the paddock for an aging stallion owned by one of our teenage helpers, but housed by us. A split-rail fence still separates the plot from the rest of the vegetable garden. The horse was such a spectacular jumper, we had to keep piling the fence rails higher until, at last, he could no longer top them. What he had wanted was the freedom of the open fields that lay beyond his paddock, but our fences there were not yet secure, so we dared not let him loose. With sorrow, he was sold — but he ended his life in glory, standing stud to a dozen fillies on a spread of rolling land that offered him all the freedom he could manage. For years, we would catch an occasional glimpse of him there — sometimes in free flight, sometimes stilled in a distant corner.

Now his paddock is our herb garden. Its plants try to run wild as the horse once did, but they have no need to leap the fences. They simply crawl underneath them and spread their roots at will. The worst of these horticultural wanderers is mint, though oregano gives it a run for its money. Every fall, I have to dig whole clusters of these herbs from neighbouring beds, and then in the spring, I have to repeat the process.

I could sink metal or plastic edging to fence in their roots, but putting barriers down into the earth defeats the purpose of making a garden in the first place, which is to create a sanctuary, not a cell. A garden with too much order in it makes me think I must go pacing there instead of strolling — hurrying through and away from it instead of sauntering into its reaches with a sense of relaxation and calmness.

A delight in herbs was instilled in me at an early age by my mother. Of course, as a child, I thought of them only as *flavours — decorations — something pleasant* to find in a soup or a salad or a sauce. As I grew older, I learned more. They were — they are — a staple not only of the best cooking but, beyond that, the source of gorgeous bouquets and pot pourri and of carefully larded additives to many kinds of food I never encountered in childhood. Also, herbs in a garden of their own offer a unique display of colour and scent.

As we extended our cultivation over time, I knew that one day I would have a herb garden but, oddly, it was the last one we created. Perhaps I was nervous of it. I had read too much, seen too many photographs, heard too much about what a herb garden *should* be. *A wild place*, on the one hand — and *a formal place* on the other. Very few people I read or talked with said: *make it your own*. And, of course, there can be no better advice about any garden. *MAKE IT YOUR OWN.* After all, it is yours.

Stone Orchard's herb garden offers sanctuary in every sense. Safe — and apart — it is cloistered but not shut away. There are views on every side of sky and of fields that rise to the distant tree lines. There is a walkway there — the traditional flagstone cross, dividing the garden into four distinct sections. Casting its shade from the south, a giant basswood occupies a corner. Until fairly recently, I could still find horsehairs embedded in its bark or caught in the ruts and runnels of the fence's top rail, where the stallion had rubbed his shoulder. Wild yellow primroses grow there now, and ferns, wood violets — a gooseberry bush. One old dog and two old cats are buried near a bench where the shade and the sunlight meet. I spend much time on this bench, watching and listening, caught in a kind of reverie. The smell of earth and of herbs and roses is very pungent — deeply pleasant, reassuring, pacifying. A bird-bath draws more insects than birds — beetles, butterflies, moths. But birds do use it. Robins will come, or sparrows; a starling arriving with a string of unruly young who always seem about to drown in the bath, they are so ungainly.

I grow four kinds of herbs in this place — herbs for their scent, their appearance, their flavour and their medicinal benefits. Some serve as the basis of salads, soups and teas. A single variety — sorrel or roquette — can provide an endless array of dishes. I once made a salad and counted into it twenty-seven different herbs. At the end of the season, late in September and all of October, there are herbs to dry and herbs to set in vinegars and jellies — herbs for scenting cupboards and drawers, herbs for use as bouquets and wreaths.

Herb vinegars are a joy to make, to use — and simply to see. I put them in whatever wine or beer bottles have the most pleas-ing shapes — and not too much pigment — and I don't preheat the vinegar. I simply label the bottle, cram in a few freshly picked leaves, fill the bottle with vinegar — cider or malt, depending on the herb — seal it up and place it on a windowsill that faces south. Time and autumn sunlight do the rest, until I have a collection of herbal infusions with countless uses — including the decoration of kitchen shelves and counters.

One of our favourite dishes is sorrel soup. On first hearing of it, one of our teenage employees asked: *sorrow soup?* Here is how it's made at Stone Orchard:

Make a béchamel sauce: gently cook 3 tbsp. butter in $^1/_3$ cup of flour for about five minutes, then add $^3/_4$ cup of milk and a generous pinch of dried basil, and continue cooking — stirring frequently — until the sauce thickens. Set aside.

Peel and cube a pound of potatoes, slice 1 large leek (or 2 large green onions) and 3 stalks of celery (including the leaves). Cook the vegetables in water, drain and set aside.

Meanwhile, wash a pound of sorrel leaves — stems removed. (I press as many leaves as I can into a four-cup measure.) Shred the leaves and cook gently in 2 tbsp. of butter, seasoning generously with salt and pepper. This will reduce them considerably, which is why you need the pound. When the leaves are soft and brownish, remove from the heat.

Now, purée the sorrel and potato mixtures in a food processor with 1 cup of chicken stock. Return the mixture to the pot in which you cooked the sorrel, add 2 or 3 more cups of stock (amount depends on the type of potato used) and cook on low while stirring in the béchamel sauce.

Season to taste, and garnish with more herbs from the garden. (Fresh chervil leaves are particularly attractive — both for the palate and the eye.)

For all its uses, our herb garden's greatest property, to me, is the uniqueness of what it offers, set aside in the larger landscape. Midsummer mornings and evenings, there is no finer pleasure than going out to sit at its heart, where half a dozen cats lift up their heads to greet me from flat, cool stones and proprietary toads sit in the shade of their toad-houses — broken clay pots I have set there for them.

Bees pass aloud — and mourning doves come to the fence with their calming lament.

This is my joy. I can dig here — plant and replant — with my hands not only in the earth, but messing in a mass of scented leaves and stalks that send me reeling. Sometimes, I come here just to sit between bouts of writing. Mornings and summer evenings, everything throws off its scent as if to say: *here is peace — enclosure — perfection*. At its gate, there is a stone dove. At its centre is the heart of Stone Orchard.

When winter comes — as it will — the garden that once was a paddock is doubly haunted, deep in the snow, by the scented remnants clinging to whatever stems I have failed to harvest and by the calls of horses out on the road as they are ridden past this place where, in some horse way, they sense the long-ago presence of one who might have been their parent. Who was, whatever else, of their kind. His, I trust, will not be the only ghost to haunt this place. I certainly mean to leave some part of me — a spirit-memento of my happiness here.

Lamma from Heaven

They were scattered beneath the wild apple and cedar trees, on the verge of the lower field — white, jewelled with dew — some of them as big as footballs. Seventy-year old Agnes Mortson saw them first.

She had accompanied us to the farm to guide us through that early time in 1964 — when we arrived a week before the furniture did. Mrs Mortson had been a girl when her family homesteaded in Saskatchewan, a few years before that part of Canada became a province in 1905. Having grown up in a sod hut, she knew all about setting up house with very little on hand. We were lucky. We had the two large beds — and the bedding — lent to us by the farm's former owner, Nelson Purvis. A visit to the village grocery store then provided us with enough orange crates to fashion a makeshift table and a few shelves.

Part of Mrs Mortson's considerable charm was her marvellous way with the language: she had already commented on the flowering "hydarange" out front. The room where Bill had already built some book shelves, she called the "liberry." Now, she pointed to the jewels under the trees and declared: "that's lamma from heaven!"

I managed the translation to "manna" but was still no wiser about what we'd found.

"Puffballs," Bill explained. Like Mrs Mortson, he had grown up in Saskatchewan, and was able to tell about these huge, apparently stemless mushrooms. "They're not all that common, and they grow so fast they seem to appear overnight. It could have been something like this that fed the Israelites in the wilderness."

We gathered three of the whitest and freshest, and carried them back to the wood stove in the kitchen. Washed, sliced and fried in butter, they became our staple food for the week — along with bread, bacon and the new potatoes that had been planted in our garden by the Purvis family.

Although we've rarely seen the puffballs again, we discovered other forms of "lamma." There were all the apple and crabapple trees that had gone wild, and that lined the lane leading down to the lower meadow and woodlot. We tried picking from them all, and found some for eating, some for pies and applesauce, and some for jellies — the latter used as the basis for a whole series of herb jellies, once my herb garden got going.

One tasty secret worth passing on, in case you don't already know it, is to lay some leaves of scented geranium on the tops of apple jellies before you seal them with wax or lids. As the jellies set, they become infused with new flavour.

That same fall, we found wild grapes twining over the fence-rows, and made our first batch of dark, delicious grape jelly, perfect on home-baked bread. We spent hours separating the fruit from the stems, cooking them down into a kind of runny jam and then tying it into an old flour sack to be hung from a cupboard door-handle, its juices dripping into one of the huge earthenware bowls we had found in the tumbledown drive-shed. We later found that many farm kitchens we visited had dark purple stains on a cupboard door — evidence of the popularity of the ubiquitous grape. We had no idea — then — what else that crop would produce in our lives.

People in the community had been wondering who we were and what we did. They hadn't yet heard that I was an aspiring novelist or that Bill was preparing documentary scripts for radio and television. All they knew was, we spent most of our time at home. *Hmm. No visible means of support — and they pick grapes.* The local conclusion was inevitable. When Bill's fairly strait-laced parents arrived from the West for their first visit, they stopped at the service station to ask directions. *Whitehead and Findley? Oh, you mean the bootleggers! Sure — you go down there and turn left . . .*

We had a fair bit of explaining to do. Especially when people started turning up at the door. Grape jelly didn't seem to be what they had in mind.

As far as our growing population of cats was concerned, the greatest boon on the property was the amount of catnip that had gone wild. Clumps of it decorated not only the garden, but the edges of neighbouring fields. The favoured clump — and the largest — was near the house; we called it "the pub," as we watched the cats, in ones, twos and threes — heading out to "tie one on." Some would collapse in blissful slumber nearby, while others staggered and wove their way across the lawns to a distant, more private shade.

One Christmas, we were given a book written by Euell Gibbons — *Stalking the Wild Asparagus*. It told us how to gather and prepare edible weeds, of which we had an overabundance. By spring, we were out in the ditches, picking day-lily buds, to be cooked and served like green beans — or shaking bullrushes over plastic bags to collect their pollen, which could be used as a startlingly yellow but delicious flour for muffins. And when we found a patch of Jerusalem artichokes down by the barn, we dug up their tubers to flavour our soups or cut into salads.

Some of Bill's radio work dealt with pioneer times in Ontario, and through this we learned of other useful products from the fields and hedgerows. Sumac bushes were plentiful all around us, and their bristly "flowers" could be soaked in water, and the water, strained, sweetened and chilled, became a delicious summer drink, not unlike pink lemonade. The "bristles" were, in fact, crystals of something very similar to malic acid, the natural substance that gives apples some of their flavour and tartness.

Not all the wild crops were for consumption. Again, with the help of one of the radio scripts, we found how to use a growth of horsetails along the railway tracks beside the river. They form jointed reeds — resembling slender, green bamboo — whose high silica content makes them excellent scouring pads for cooking pots.

And for decoration, there was material all around us. Bill's niece Lorraine made us a beautiful Christmas wreath out of intertwined grape vines. It became a fixture on the studio wall — looking down on urns filled with dried plants such as the honesty growing among all the resident Victorian perennials. Honesty is also called "the money plant," as its round, silvery seed pods resemble coins. Then, too, we made good use of the great fronds and heads of pampas grass, brought from a friend's garden, and soon spreading all around one end of the pond.

One spring, we tried serving milkweed buds as vegetables, changing the cooking water twice to eliminate the bitterness of the "milk." We always shared the plants with Monarch butterflies, until municipal spraying of "noxious weeds," part of a pest-control program, made rarities out of both milkweed and Monarchs. In recent years we have left them all for the butterflies, they have become so scarce.

Fortunately, we have devised a gentler means of "pest control." Corn, we found, is "manna for raccoons." Every year it would disappear as soon as it was ripe — until we began planting *our* crop right beside the dog pen, with another small corn patch on the other side of the house. There, the raccoons find it on their way up from the river. Discouraged by an occasional shout from the dogs, they leave our cobs entirely alone.

Recently, the raccoons discovered a new kind of manna — or perhaps they call it *lamma*. This is the kibble we put out on the porch for our cats. We watch in the evenings: the two kinds of animals, one wild, the other domesticated, feeding side by side — with a raccoon matron taking a kibble break while the younger cats entertain her kits.

At such moments, it is hard not to think of this place as a kind of paradise. Or, at least, a Peaceable Kingdom.

Fencelines

If good fences make good neighbours, does it follow that bad fences make bad neighbours? Not necessarily, but bad fences can certainly make bad farmers. Some years ago, new people moved in next door to *Stone Orchard* and, never having run a farm, they decided to take down most of their fences, including the line that ran along the road. It was astonishing — odd — as if they had set their own barns on fire or ploughed good corn into the ground. There was never an explanation. They simply pulled them down. Perhaps it was aesthetic. Who could tell. At any rate, off their cattle went — up the road and through the woods and into other people's barnyards. This happened day after day almost all of one whole summer, until it seemed that, in spite of endless pleading, cajoling and threatening, our neighbours were simply immune to reason. They were, we concluded, addicted to pulling down fences. In the long run, all we could do was laugh when yet again we would wake to find one of their cattle standing on our back porch waiting, so it seemed, for admittance to the house — with a gift of lettuces torn from our vegetable garden.

Sadly, there were tragic consequences to this comic turn. Our neighbours finally took down the fence that had stood for years between the river and the meadow where their cattle had at last been confined for the winter months. On a mid-January morning, just three days later, thirty-five cattle and calves went out onto the ice and were drowned when it gave way beneath them. Most baffling of all was the fact that even after these wasted deaths, the fence was not replaced. When we were told of this tragedy, it was related as a kind of triumph. The young man who informed us was, strangely, smiling. "It doesn't matter," he said. "They were insured." Only then did the wreck of the fences take on its true meaning.

At last — and mercifully, for all concerned — our neighbours decided that "farming" was not their calling and not their joy. They gave up the enterprise altogether and, after further disasters, they moved away.

Their determined folly, however, had reinforced our own sense of responsibility. Not being fence builders ourselves, we decided it would be useful to barter for the making and maintenance of Stone Orchard's fencelines. We have never regretted it. In return for the use of our fields and barn, neighbouring farmers Leonard Griffin and his son, Keith, not only mended our split-rail fences and erected new ones, they also provided us with the stone foundations of two fallen barns — and it was with these stones that we built the wall that stands today between our house and the road.

It is wonderful to see how other of these foundations have persisted over the years since they were first set in place — some as long ago as the 1830s. We tend to forget — and it's a sad forgetfulness — that all the houses and barns of those early years, like ours, were erected and finished without the benefit of modern power equipment. Every brick and every board and shingle was either fashioned on the premises or brought in overland from the mills and yards to the south. No trucks — no tractors — no trains. In time, of course, all of these came into being, but the first influx of Irish, Scots and English pioneers arrived with nothing but hand tools, horses, oxen and themselves. And so, they set about erecting whatever they needed — the buildings and the fences.

Even as our own stones were being laid, I could not resist the memory of Robert Frost's "Mending Wall" and his eloquent plea for a world without barriers. The poem tells us: "Something there is that doesn't love a wall." And Frost says: "Before I built a wall I'd ask to know/ What I was walling in or walling out . . ." Always a good question — but it did not prevent the wall we have from rising, nor the fences that come to its corners. I will admit, there is an element here at Stone Orchard of walling in the past and of trying to hold the future at bay. It will come — and has begun its arrival already — too quickly, with its invasions of snowmobiles and all-terrain vehicles. And yet, Stone Orchard is not a fortress. We could not abide a fortress. Along the wall there are gates that have now stood open so long that vines have grown on them and tethered them in that position to the earth.

Weathered cedar rails zig-zag around most of our fields — although some stretches are still marked by the barbed wire that was strung before we came here. The very mention of the word *fence* brings a medley of images to mind: a parade of cats tightrope-walking along the top rail as we exercise the dogs; tufts of coarse, dark fur caught on the barbs of the wire that surrounded the vegetable garden — proof that Len's sister Julie really did see a black bear run across the road and into our garden; the plastic model of a human brain, perched on a cedar rail in a blizzard, as a horse runs through the falling snow beyond it — one of the camera shots in a documentary Bill wrote about human thought and perception.

Cedar rails — commonplace in the countryside — are prized by city folk. One couple with whom we had been friends for years came out to collect some of our spare rails to use in their Toronto garden. We were all short of time — our friends anxious to beat rush-hour traffic, Bill and I struggling with writing deadlines. Just as our friends were about to leave, the wife spotted the profusion of lilac blossoms in the front yard. Could she take some home? Indeed, she could — and I went to get my new pruning shears for her to use. She decided not to wait — and began tearing branches off the huge old lilac bush, stripping the bark right down the trunk as she worked. When I got back with the shears, she took them, marched over to our new picnic table and — explaining that lilacs last longer if you "bash" the ends of their stems — she proceeded to do so with such vigour that the picnic table was badly gouged and the pruning shears broke in two. A bad day — but somehow, the friendship survived.

We have stiles set out along the fence-rows. We put them there many years ago when our parents were still alive, telling ourselves that "old folks" needed all the assistance they could get. Fair enough. I use them almost every day myself, now. The fences themselves — or some of them — are more than one hundred years old: snake fences, stump fences. Pioneer fences. It seems impossible, but there are split rails here that were cut from the woods in the 1840s. A good fence can last a lifetime and more.

Leonard Griffin, now long dead, introduced Bill and me to the use of *neighbour* as a verb. "He neighbours well," Leonard would say — even of someone who otherwise displeased him. To have it said that you neighbour well is the highest compliment you can be given in a farming community. And your commitment to your fencing makes a large contribution to your reputation.

The fences Leonard and Keith made for us are, in some way, a fitting memorial to them both — though Keith is still very much alive. Their fences will outlast us all, so long as there are cattle to be managed here. Now, when I ask what it is I am "walling in or walling out," I think the answer has something to do with time. Fences have a way of confining time's passage with their geometry, but there is always a gate that lets time in and out and stiles that let it pass from field to field.

I caught a glimpse, once, of Leonard Griffin taking bales of hay to his cattle, stranded at a distance after a blizzard. He was standing up behind his horses on an old-fashioned sledge with the hay piled all around him. And as if my eye had been a camera, it took a snapshot of him there: this time-worn old man who had been a farmer all his life, and his horses and his sledge, passing along the fence-rows he had raised. This is what I want to wall in here — time's images, etched and indelible. And I would wall out all forgetfulness. If I could.

The Blue Barn

It rises across the road from Stone Orchard, a landmark in more ways than one. You hear people say: "just go along past the blue barn . . ." And I swear that airline pilots use it as well. You can watch the jets coming in from overseas on a summer day, apparently responding to the order: "there it is; start your turn . . ." In fact, Bill and I have witnessed this from the air. Flights going to Toronto from Montreal definitely bank right at the blue barn.

For me, it is a literary landmark — my Ark, while I was writing *Not Wanted on the Voyage*, a novel about Noah and the Flood. I used to spend whole nights in there, listening to the discourse of hens and the raiding parties of mice in the granary. I slept in the hay lofts above the midnight shuffling of cattle, pigs and horses as the weathered sides of our sanctuary heaved and sighed in the wind. It was wonderful. What I got from those nights in that huge, creaking structure was the voice of the Ark itself, and of its passengers. One aspect of those times which I found both fascinating and deeply moving was the "dialogue" of the animals around me as we passed together through the dark. That they speak to one another is undeniable. That they speak of matters we may never fathom now seems to me to be equally undeniable.

Bill and I were the ones who painted the barn blue — perhaps *because* it was to be my Ark. When we had first heard the property was for sale, we were sorry — not to say worried — that the only interested buyers were developers, who looked at its rolling contours and saw a potential gravel pit. Everyone else saw a classic Georgian brick house and a great red barn on hills that were bounded on the north by the Beaver River. It was one of the last of the working farms on that side of the road. Its owner, Leonard Griffin, was suffering from health problems and had to be persuaded to retire, after which he and Jean, his wife, moved into the village. Consequently, Bill and I plunged into debt in order to buy the farm, basically to save it from the contractors. Once I was living and writing there, we called it *Arkwright*.

In a way, the blue barn is also an historical landmark — but sadly, one that is not unique. It's an L-shaped barn, and part of the "L" was moved to its present position from a farm across the river. Leonard Griffin had bought that farm in the 1930s after its former owner had hanged himself — in the barn. There had been times — too many times — when the rigours of farming life were overwhelming. Another such tragedy had occurred earlier, just down the road from us. Shortly after the turn of the century, a young couple had no sooner set up a farming operation than their barn burned down — before they'd even had a chance to insure it. It happened only two weeks after they'd moved in. The husband never recovered from this dreadful mishap — financially, or in spirit. And he, too — having attempted to drown his sorrows in alcohol — took his own life. This was long before our time, but his wife, whom we met, took on a legendary status as a dignified survivor. She continued to live in her marriage-house until her death, when she was over ninety.

Such stories made us deeply aware of how fortunate we have been — to have had the many benefits of rural living, without the pressures and disasters that are so often visited on members of any farming community: fires, crop failures, accidents and weather.

Finally, after years of maintenance and some renovation, and after the best of our tenants had moved elsewhere, I took up residence at Arkwright in the mid-1980s. That was when we painted the barn blue. It was also the time when construction of a new wing at Stone Orchard was interrupting the writing of that novel about the Ark. The consequent move across the road let me see, firsthand, just what it means to live the life of a farmer.

But I wasn't the one who had to live it. I was too busy writing, while every day — and I mean *every* day of the year — Keith and Catherine Griffin, Leonard's son and daughter-in-law, would arrive to do the necessary chores. Now, they rented the fields on both our properties. Morning and evening, winter and summer: checking on the feed, dealing with the barn's temperamental well, helping with the delivery of a new calf. On bitterly cold February mornings, I would watch them chopping through the ice on the pond with axes because the plumbing in the barn was frozen. I have never in my whole life seen two people work harder, longer or more relentless hours.

When the construction was over, I moved back home to Stone Orchard, and soon we sold that second farm and its Georgian house to Len Collins. Now he was planning on adding a cow-calf operation to his work as a carpenter, so he moved his family in and set about building up a herd of Limousins, which shared the barn with Dolly, the pony Len had had since being a boy.

We, too, had a horse in that barn — the second one we'd kept there. Some years before, we had heard from a young friend of an animal in distress — and so we bought her and had her stabled and pastured at what was then the Leonard Griffin farm. Our only slight regret was that our new filly came equipped with a name. I'm afraid it was a bit difficult for two writers to admit their horse was called *Flicka*. It was not unlike having to say you had a dog called *Spot* or a cat called *Mew*. Still, Flicka had eight long years of pleasant retirement there, before old age and lameness finally overtook her.

Our present horse was a draught animal whose working days were sadly over. He had foundered pulling stone weights in a competition and had been fated for the knacker's. And so, we made the same arrangement with young Len we'd had with the Griffins: the horse, a gelding, would live at Arkwright, and I would not only have visiting and feeding privileges, I would also administer whatever medications I could. A horse can smell medications a mile away and they had to be mitigated with apples, sugar cubes and carrots. But again, we had a problem over the name. This fellow was called *Bill*. You can imagine the conversational confusions this produced. *Bill was rolling on his back in the clover this morning!* Len's children finally solved the problem. There was *Bill*, with whom I shared Stone Orchard — and there was *Bill-the-Horse*, who shared their fields.

Once Len got his Limousin herd going, he told his wife, Anne, and the three children: "these are farm animals, not pets. They will not have names, only numbers." This was Len's strategy to avoid strong attachments to young calves or old cows who were being shipped off to slaughter.

Did it work? Well — the first time we had dinner with the Collinses after the livestock operation was in full swing, Len said: "bring your drinks, and come on out to see the herd." The cattle were in the field behind the blue barn. While Anne and the children watched with smiling approval, Len introduced us to the cows and calves, one by one. "This is my favourite," he said. "Number thirty-three. She's the gentlest lady of the whole lot. Hello, thirty-three. Hello, there, girl . . ." (vigorous rubbing of thirty-three's forehead). "And this is her newborn calf, number forty-two. Lovely forty-two. Isn't he something?" So it went, down the whole roster of "unnamed" animals . . .

Still, off to market they went — and off they continue to go. But not without the long hours of labour that I had witnessed first with Keith and Cath — the constant need to feed and medicate and watch and supervise. That need sometimes involves the whole Collins family. Cattle farmers have to deal with back-breaking births in the middle of the night and the heart-breaking deaths of sickly calves who won't nurse. And with drought one year and torrential rains the next, either of which will beat the corn to the ground and ruin the hay crop. On top of which there is always the precarious state of the futures and livestock markets.

It's the family farmer whose endless labour lies at the basis of our food supply, whether he be raising beasts or she be raising crops. It's the farmer who must cope with the reality of weather, the unpredictability of prices, the veterinary bills and the competition of the gigantic operations of Agrobiz. When I watch Len and Anne at work or think about Keith and Cath, I wonder how much of our attention and support the farmers of this country receive.

This way, the blue barn became another kind of landmark for me, because it was living in its daily presence — outside it, inside it — that brought me to the answer. How much support do we give the family farmers of our country? Considering what they provide for us and for the world at large — not nearly enough. In fact, if truth be told, beyond symbolic gestures — we offer nothing. Not only that — we turn and look the other way while dining.

The Field
across the Road

For more than thirty years Bill and I have been eating most of our meals at the kitchen table, and at some point in every meal, a silence falls as we gaze out the window at the field across the road. During winter lunches, if the snow begins to fly, we watch the field and its animals do a slow fade to white. Every spring, we wait to catch the first glimpse of ground-hogs, basking in the sun — or of a red fox, trotting through the greening grass. Summer brings Len Collins's herd of cattle — stepping like Chinese dancers, with a bull whose back has been drawn by someone with a ruler. In their midst, Dolly, the ancient pony who clearly thinks she is a cow.

There is a theory — widely, though not universally, held — that the presence of a horse or pony, mule or donkey in a herd of cattle or sheep acts as a deterrent to marauding dogs or wolves. In Len's case, this seems to hold true for, even though timber wolves and the odd wild pack of dogs have existed in our area, none of his cattle has ever been attacked. I have also noted other farms in our vicinity where mules, donkeys and

horses are pastured with cattle or sheep, and nothing unto-
ward has occurred, though one unprotected herd of cattle
nearby has suffered at least three such incidents. An interesting fact — though "non-scientific" in terms of proof.

Sometimes, we cross the road and walk through the field to
the river that forms its northern boundary. There, we sit on
the rocks and watch the turtles sunning themselves, wood
ducks foraging, or the heron fishing for minnows. Often, this
excursion means threading our way through herds of cows —
and one day our eldest cat, Mouse, went with us. At that time,
one of the cows was nursing its calf. Mouse was mesmerized.
Could she smell the milk? We don't know — but she began to
purr and, arching her back, to rub up against the cow's legs.
From that day on Mouse loved cattle. We would see her out
in the field, wandering among them, treating them with
exactly the same affectionate expectation she showed to us as
we carried food to her bowl.

Mouse also loved pigs. When Leonard Griffin still lived
across the road, he would let the sows lead their piglets down
into a gully in the field, to wallow by the pond in the mud. If
Mouse happened to be among the cats accompanying us on a
walk at such a time, she would join the piglets, leaning in and
walking shoulder to shoulder with one of them. Then cat,
piglets and people would watch as the sow heaved a great sigh
of pleasure and sank down into the cooling mud — until all
that could be seen of her was two ears, two contented eyes
and a pink snout.

On a sunny day one early spring, Len and I were grooming
the horses in that field — not far from the yard of the blue
barn. Len had his pony, Dolly — and I had Bill-the-Horse.
Tess was with us, too — Len's black Labrador, lying in what
remained of the snow, watching with interest as we plied our
brushes and curry-combs.

Suddenly, Tess shot off across the field. She had spotted a vixen, carrying a fatally early-rising groundhog. The fox was heading back to her den which, we knew, was just over the crest of a rise to the west. When she saw who was headed in her direction, the vixen dropped her prey and tore off over the rise. Tess had blundered into deep snow, where it drifted in the lee of a hill. By then, she could see the fox had disappeared and, deciding she had done her duty, she made her way back to us. Her sea-otter's eyes were smiling, her tail slowly wagging. Obviously, she was pleased with herself for having cleared the field. She flopped down once more and began to bite the snow from between the pads of her paws.

Thus, Tess failed to see what we then witnessed. The vixen cautiously appeared on the horizon, scouted the situation and then, belly to the snow, moved swiftly down to the abandoned groundhog carcass, picked it up and headed home. Very soon after that her two kits were seen enjoying the meal she had brought them, while the vixen sat beside them, looking down at us. The word *insouciance* occurred to me. *You guys don't know the half of it*, her posture informed us. I would agree. Talk about an end run!

It was in a corner of this field that I once sat and watched a calf being born. Years later, I wrote about this birth in *The Piano Man's Daughter*, in which the title character, Lily, was also born in that corner. It was where she had been conceived and where she entered the world. It was also where her character entered my mind. The field was the centre of Lily's childhood, and it remained with her as an image until the day she died. The village to the north is now called Cannington, but until 1878 it was known as McCaskill's Mills, and in the book that is the name I gave to Lily's village.

Draped in its winter white — as now — the field also entered another piece of writing. In the 1970s, Bill and I were hired to create a CBC television series based on Pierre Berton's two superb books about the building of the CPR — *The National Dream* and *The Last Spike* .

Except for a twenty-two-second recap of how the previous episode had ended, the final episode was completely edited. All we needed was a single shot of a Métis figure, lying dead in the snow — over which the narration would tell of the outbreak of the 1885 Riel Rebellion. The problem was, the film crews and costume people had long dispersed.

In desperation, we spoke to one of the series cameramen, Rudi Kovanic, who had worked for years with Bill on "The Nature of Things." Rudi agreed to drive up to Stone Orchard in order to shoot the missing moment. It was up to us to provide a suitably costumed Métis corpse.

This was to be me — ex-actor, player of many corpses over time in my days as a theatre walk-on and a television extra. Rummaging in closets and drawers, I found an old fringed buckskin jacket and a bright red woven sash. Rudi parked his CBC van in front of our stone wall, and we all went into the field across the road. I arranged myself in a "frozen-death" position. Bill dribbled shovelfuls of snow over me until I looked as if I had been lying there for days. He then began to work out the shot with Rudi. With the camera thirty feet away, it was to be a slow pan lasting the required twenty-two seconds. Commencing with the feet of the corpse, it would end on an artfully raised "frozen" hand. This was to be my master-stroke.

ACTION!

I closed my eyes and held my breath.

Rudi totally ignored my posed hand and began noting other possibilities: the silhouette of distant trees — the gorgeous roll of the land — a flight of birds. *No*, Bill told him — *all we have is twenty-two seconds*. While they argued, I was suffocating, having been forbidden to breathe because the vapour of my breath would have proved I was alive. Finally, I had to exhale — using the moment to explode with loud complaints. I was not about to become a real corpse, even for the sake of art.

Finally, Rudi was convinced to shoot the original twenty-two-second version, and I again assumed my breathless pose.

By now, however, trucks and cars had begun to gather along the fence-row. Drivers and passengers hurried into the ditch. The sight of a CBC van and cameraman filming a dead body was irresistible. *Murder? Suicide? Was this to be on the evening news? Maybe we'll be interviewed on camera!* But then — alas — the body stood up and brushed off its snow.

We won't be seen on TV after all, someone said bitterly. I felt as if I should apologize for being alive. The cars and trucks, reoccupied, were driven off.

This, it so happened, was Timothy Findley's farewell performance on camera. A career had died, if not a man. And when "The National Dream" is next aired, as it has been every few years, you may see for yourselves the living dead — in the field across the road.

Constant Companions

*S*TONE ORCHARD, FOR US, HAS ALWAYS MEANT *having animals. It has been more or less a menagerie of pets, strays and visitors of all kinds — each of them welcomed, some of them remaining with us for life.*

What's in a Name?

We called this place *Stone Orchard* as a tribute to one of my favourite writers, Anton Chekhov. His masterpiece, *The Cherry Orchard*, might have been set here — barring our lack of cherry trees. The climate simply won't accommodate them. What we do have, though, is stones; every ploughing, every digging, every frost that rises brings them to the surface.

The trouble is, no sooner had we settled on the name than someone asked us why we had chosen to live in a graveyard. It seems the local inhabitants long ago decided that cemeteries were also stone orchards! Well, we could accommodate that. Our parents' ashes — and now, my brother's — are scattered here beneath the trees. Four great dogs are buried in the flower-beds: Maggie and Hooker, Belle and Berton. And throughout the gardens are the graves of more than a hundred cats — each with a fondly remembered personality and name.

We have only two rules about the animals' names: Rule #1: *don't put them in my novels*. Three of our first cat's initial litter became characters in my first novel, *The Last of the Crazy People*, and all three had perished before the book was finished. I've since wondered if I could hire myself out as a literary hit-man.

If enemies, you've got 'em,
Give me their names
And you've not 'em.
All that I ask is a fee,
Twelve million bucks and you're free!

On the other hand, I'm a pacifist. Save your money, work out your differences and we'll all survive.

Rule #2: *don't use connected names*. Ruff *and* Tumble: Ruff became one of our first casualties on the road. Smokey's kittens, named for cigarettes — Whiff, Belvedere, du Maurier and Black Cat: all four were slaughtered by a marauding tom. This happens, but rarely. Rogue tom cats, as with some other species, will kill the young they find — perhaps in a bid for supremacy and survival.

Some of the cats have been named for the creatures they resembled: Sparrow, Kittiwake, Phoebe and Greylag. Some for feathers — others for fur: Mouse and Mole, Rabbit and Fawn, Buffalo and Bear. Then there were Trout and Turtle, Cricket and Moth. Some showed human traits: Gulliver, who travelled; Jason, who ventured; Ezra, who pondered; Barbra, who sang — and not incidentally, also shared Ms Streisand's classic profile.

Many of our cats were born here; many others simply arrived, either by wandering in or having been dropped off by people who wanted — for one negligent reason or another — to be rid of them. These were often whole litters of kittens — or a pregnant female.

We discovered one such female on the back porch — hugely swollen with soon-to-be-born progeny. To our puzzlement, she retained her swollen shape for months afterwards — and consequently, so we were to learn, until the end of her life. So we called her Mother. This, it turned out, was a grave mistake.

In order to understand why, you have to know two other things about Stone Orchard. Firstly, we had assigned one-half of the woodshed as a winter home for the outdoor cats. In the summer, it housed the swimming pool filtration system, but once the cold weather set in, we would cover the floor with straw and install a kind of incubator made of galvanized tin, heated by a suspended infra-red bulb. The cats had their own entrance to this haven, through an opening nicely sheltered from the prevailing wind.

Secondly, you have to know that at the time of Mother's advent, we fed the birds from a table-sized feeder, situated just outside the kitchen window, where we could watch the daily action. One part of this action included the occasional hunting foray by one of the cats, who would lie patiently motionless for birds to walk into its mouth. But birds are smart and, of course, this never happened. Another action featured Mother, the cat, who loved to use the build-up of seed husks as a litter box. Both activities were firmly discouraged by whichever of us happened to be watching — but in the latter case, not always with great success.

Now, the story moves to Toronto where, one winter morning, Bill and I are on the subway, heading off to our various appointments. It is one of those cold, early mornings when nobody seems to want to talk very much. Thus, the car is relatively quiet, and we seem to be the only two having a conversation. The subject today is the recurring problem of competition between the birds and one of the cats for that precious spread of seeds. It is Bill who first mentions it.

"Honestly, Tiff, I don't know what to do. Did you notice? Just as we were about to leave, Mother shat in the bird feeder again."

"I know," I reply. "I think we'll just have to lock her in the cat-house until she learns to behave."

We both then lean back to ponder the problem, slowly becoming aware of what is happening around us. Copies of *The Globe and Mail* are lowered. Accusing eyes are turned towards us, faces registering a mixture of horror and puzzlement.

Who are these barbarian brothers who treat their mother thus???

Needless to say, this ends our conversation.

As you might imagine, you can't make a move around Stone Orchard without encountering a cat. A few live in the house, where they lie on the tops of shelves and underneath the throw-rugs, waiting to ambush hands that reach for books and feet that pass along the hallways. They monitor every mouthful of food we eat while turning up their noses at every bit of cat food set in their dishes. *Cat food is CAT FOOD! We want yours!* They also rummage with wild abandon in their boxes, scattering kitty litter every way from Sunday, walking away entirely aloof: *what — me create this chaos? Never . . .*

Most of them live in the garden, with access, in the winter, to the heated woodshed. We once had an outdoor cat named Trot. Given her bouncy gait, she was first called Trottie — until we lopped the end off her name the year the hay-reaper lopped off the latter part of her tail. After that, she spent a good deal of time sitting down, alone. Cats, if mutilated, have a mournful sense of dignity about their loss. Then, an aging, wondrous creature, worn and torn in the wars, turned up one day and sat down beside her. Seeing his raggedness, and the errant gleam in his eye, we called him Quixote. Trot became his Dulcinea. Both of them had been neutered, so this was not a question of rampant lust. Or lust of any kind. It was simply *chivalry — for cats.*

No matter where you looked, you were bound to see them. Trot in a pool of sunlight, the Don in a doze at her feet. Trot in a quest for water, Quixote at the reeded edge of the pond, scaring off the frogs. Trot's evening stroll atop the split-rail fence — Quixote sedately following after, his tail an upright lance. I saw them once by moonlight, sitting side by side on a stile. It might have been an illustration for a love story. But, in the human sense, it was not. We've heard that *animals are just like us*. What about: *we are just like them*? Would it were so. When was the last time you went out and sat with someone on a stile in the moonlight? *Being bonded*, I came to understand, is not like *being in love*. It is more profound than that. The year Trot died, Quixote left Stone Orchard. Eventually, we found his body down in the woods. We buried him there. It had been his choice.

I've often wondered — do the cats name each other? Do they name us? Can their various greetings be translated into: *Hello, Two-foot. Hello, Stumbler. Noisemaker. Feeder. Hello, He-who-opens-gates*. And *greetings, She-who-makes-a-lap* . . . ?

Names are touchstones. Names are flags, signalling the magic of unique identity — the wonder of individuality. They are a shorthand code that can summon the image of a creature — whole and absolute. That is why there are no gravestones in our "stone orchard." The speaking of names is monument enough to all those who rest here.

Cat People

When we arrived in the Cannington area in 1964, accompanied by seven purring beasts, we were perceived — correctly — as cat people. We soon discovered others, such as Gertrude Graham, widow of a former Fire Chief in the village and once the moving force in the Women's Auxiliary of the Fire Brigade. Gertie's death, like her life, was widely honoured in the community. We all had fond memories of the Graham porches and gardens on Laidlaw Street, sprinkled with cats of all sizes and ages — many of them, calicos — whose numbers were always a matter of uncertainty and wonder. Possibly even to Gertie, herself. *Where on earth did they all come from?*

Our own numbers quickly grew. Pregnancies. Strays wandering in. Then, litters of weaned kittens would appear mysteriously in the front garden. At first we welcomed these anonymous gifts, but as they continued we became nervous every time we heard a car slowing down in the night. Especially if it was a Volkswagen. I don't know why, but several — not to say most — of our newcomers arrived in such a vehicle. We certainly came to wish for some indication of how many in each "drop." I cannot count the number of "dark and stormy" nights I've spent tromping around the yard in the dark — often in blizzards or cloudbursts — making sure there wasn't one more kitten to be found.

Some of the most appealing arrivals have come on their own — aging toms, veterans of a lifetime of raw, romantic battles. Each has had tremendous dignity — a kind of reluctant aloofness that had to be worn away with affectionate persistence. Sometimes it took a year or more before we could finally make physical contact. But after that first touch, there would inevitably be an orgy of rubbing up against legs, and of ears and jaws proffered for petting.

Given the feline population at Stone Orchard, it seemed inevitable that friends and employees — even dedicated dog people — would also become cat people. Certainly Len Collins, who loves most animals, exhibited both skill and heart in handling our meowing crew.

If there were a pet-owner's medal for bravery beyond the call of duty, Len would certainly have earned it the day we asked him to take one of the old toms down to the veterinary clinic to be neutered. Since our burgeoning cat community was large, we neutered them all as soon as we could — both to control their numbers and to cut down on infighting. With battle-scarred toms, of course, this process had to wait for some breakthrough to trust and touching. And the moment had finally arrived for a surgical tranquillizer to be given to an old boy named, for his appearance, Harelip. He was the only one of two old males who could even be approached.

Unfortunately, on the day of the clinic appointment, both Bill and I had to be in Toronto. This meant that Len would have to single-handedly get Harelip into the cat carrier and down to the vets. When we got home that night, we were glad to discover a note assuring us *all went well.*

It had, in fact, gone better than any of us realized. When Len brought the cat home the next day, the animal he released was not Harelip, but our fiercest new arrival — unnamed, as yet, and up to that point, having never allowed any of us anywhere near him. If Harelip was difficult, this cat was impossible. Len bore the scars for weeks and was never willing to tell us how he managed to get him into the carrier. And, for reasons we dare not imagine, none of the vets has revealed what happened at the clinic. At any rate, the result was a friendlier, happier cat who, in spite of his neutered state, spent the rest of his days at the top of the heap. *King, Emperor* or what you will, he was supreme. We called him Caesar.

It took only five years for our cat numbers to peak at thirty-six. Now, it's settled down to a manageable twelve. All along, our local veterinary clinic has been staffed by a series of godsends, although our first encounter was not auspicious. When one of our original cats became ill, I telephoned Doctor Wrex Groves — long since retired — who listened with interest and sympathy while I detailed the symptoms. He asked where the animal was at the present time. I replied, truthfully: "right here, on my lap." There was a long pause. Up until that moment, Doctor Groves had been under the impression I was talking not about a cat — but a calf.

Vets, as is true of doctors who deal with human beings, are a race apart. They have a gift of patience — you should pardon the pun — that is awe-inspiring. Without them none of us would survive with half the ease that we do, in spite of pain — in spite of panic.

The clinic's next owner, Doctor Al Bowness — among the greater godsends — has recently sold the clinic to two of his former colleagues, a young married couple named Mike Stephenson and Debbie Davies.

Mike's amused gaze and benign moustache belie his ability to tackle just about anything — such as, recently, having to lasso and immobilize a crazed, pregnant cow and deliver her calf. "Doctor Debbie," as she's now known, specializes in the care of small animals — including miniature hedgehogs, Vietnamese pigs, the occasional squirrel or loon — and dogs and cats. Thanks to Debbie, pet owners in our community still receive the benefits of house-calls — a privilege for which we have, on stressful occasions, been extremely grateful. Somehow, our arrival at the clinic with thirty or more cats requiring their annual injections was an event considered too fraught with turmoil, even for the most experienced vet. And so, for most of our time in the community, Brelmar Clinic has sent someone to us when it was time for animal shots. Now, we are particularly lucky, since Stone Orchard lies on the well-beaten path between Debbie and Mike's house and their clinic. As well as the pleasure of the occasional social visit, we also gain the privilege of having our animals taken to the clinic, when necessary, and ultimately delivered home again.

In the country, of course, Doctor Deb must also be adept at handling farm animals. And their owners. Some regard a female vet with doubt and misgiving; others, with special interest. Deb tells of one encounter during her early years of practice, near Ottawa. While she was perched beside him on a bale of hay, making out her bill, the aging farmer in question expressed the hope that her fee would not be too high. He reinforced his sentiment with a proprietary hand on her thigh. Not missing a beat in her notations, Doctor Debbie casually replied: "the cost goes up a hundred bucks every second that hand stays there!" The hand was removed at once.

Among our favourite cat people is a woman who used to spend her days in what we once viewed as the heart of Cannington. This was our local service station, then run by Carl Mark and his partner, Bernice Heise. Sadly, Carl died not long ago, and the Esso station is closed. In its day, however, providing fuel and mechanical expertise was only a part of the service. Morning visits also included local "news" and weather forecasts. If you wanted to know what was what, you asked Bernice — who had also turned the office into a haven for Cannington's "old boys," both human and feline. Surrounded at several levels by cardboard nesting boxes, a gathering of local ancients could always be found on the benches, sipping coffee, chatting with Bernice and Carl, while each of the boxes was the blanketed haven of some battle-scarred tom — all of them strays who, thanks to Bernice, had finally "come home" to safety, warmth and regular meals.

Until the station is sold, Bernice still provides shelter there for both kinds of "old boys," although some of the senior cats have joined her in her apartment. Most of her time is now spent looking after Jane Elizabeth, whose parents — Doctors Debbie and Mike — spend most of their time at the clinic or out on calls. It is interesting to note that Jane's arrival has in no way diminished the number of dogs and cats — many of them, strays — being sheltered and fed at her parents' home. It, too, is haven.

During a recent stay in our other house in France, we were adopted by a stray kitten — a real charmer. What else could she be? Charm is an art with cats. None of our neighbouring cat-people claimed her. This was problematical. A home had to be found before our return to Canada. There were immediate offers from our neighbours of a litter box, cat toys and feeding dishes. And just before we left, a permanent home was located for the cat. We may not always be so lucky. Perhaps, on every future absence from Stone Orchard, our luggage should include the basic cat necessities — just in case.

Old Dogs
Teach New Tricks

Dogs spend all their lives training people, and by the time they're old — the dogs, I mean — they've pretty well got us doing things their way. Buy the wrong kind of kibble? A couple of disdainful sniffs, a few reproachful looks and you start buying the *right* kind. Be late for a feeding or an outing? You hear about it. Loudly. This is why dogs hate the way we change our clocks every fall — it delays everything an hour.

Since coming to Stone Orchard in 1964, Bill and I have lived with, and been trained by three pairs of dogs. Our first dog was single — for a while. Until she went into heat. Then she taught us that it's not a good idea to shut an eager female up in the house. The lesson cost one battered door and two destroyed carpets — but only three broken windows.

That was Maggie, and when she thought we were a little slow in finding homes for the resultant pups — there were nine of them — she started taking them around the neighbourhood, herself — carting them dangling from her mouth and dropping a couple at the next farm down the road, three at the house on the corner and so on. Finally, as pup by pup, all of them found their way home, we were persuaded to join in this relocation scheme, until only one remained. This was Hooker, who stayed with us for the rest of his life.

It was Maggie and Hooker who taught me something about the private lives of dogs. I was curious. What do dogs do at night, for example, when they're alone? All our dogs have lived in a large chain-link pen. The sleeping quarters are in a low-roofed hut with plenty of straw bedding. It had been a goose house. I crawled in once and spent the night with the dogs. The first thing I learned was that at no time were both dogs asleep. After I was established in the straw beside the hut's only window — a privilege they accorded me — Maggie went out, dug up a favourite bone and had a midnight gnaw. Dare I say "gnawsh?" When she came back, Hooker left for a while, to shout at the raccoons who were catching frogs down at the pond. In he came and out she went. That's the way it was, all night long. I didn't sleep a wink, but happily, I was fascinated. And when it started to get light — they both went outside. I followed, and learned how to greet the dawn. *You face the east — and you bow*. First Maggie, then Hooker. Then me. We bowed to the rising sun.

Occasionally, Bill and I got to be the teachers. When Maggie died, Hooker was inconsolable — mute until we sat with him one morning, threw back our heads and howled. At that, Hooker sat up, raised his own head — and gave voice to his loneliness. It could be said that we sang a lament. After that, all was well.

A few weeks later, the new pup arrived. A malamute — Belle (Klondike Belle, officially) — a silver minx who knew from the start how to charm us into subservience. She ate first; she got the biggest bone; she led the daily walk. Hook was smitten — for life. And when he died, another malamute pup arrived. This was Belle's half-brother Berton — who grew up to be as big and just as magical a son of the Klondike as his namesake, Pierre. When Berton, the dog — part wolf and part Siberian husky — stood at the fence on his hind legs, he was almost two metres tall. No mere humans were going to dictate to *him*. Soon, he was leading our pack.

He also taught us — for all his hugeness — just how gentle apparently intimidating animals can be. One Saturday, an old friend arrived — Rudi Kovanic. He brought his companion, Haruko Flower, her two children, her mother and their two "dogs." Introduced as dogs, they looked in all honesty more like friendly rodents. Hamsters, perhaps. Or guinea pigs. In fact, they were very small Jack Russell terriers. And I mean *very* small. Bite-size.

In the course of the visit, it was decided we would all go for a walk. Bill and I immediately suggested that we not include our own dogs on this excursion; we were not at all sure how they'd react to the minuscule canine visitors who had already proved to be noisome. Rudi assured us, however, that his terriers had completely won over every large dog they had ever encountered. So, we all went out to the dog pen in order to facilitate this friendly encounter. All, that is, except me. Visitors or not, I had a deadline to meet, and went upstairs to my study.

No sooner had I sat down than the most unholy racket started outside. By the time I got downstairs to the kitchen, there was Haruko's mother, very small — and very upset. She looked at me with wild eyes, attempted a smile and said: *ah . . . your dog . . . kills our dog*. She then bowed — entirely formal, entirely Japanese — and added, somewhat enigmatically: *thank you.*

Outside, I learned what had really happened. The minute he was let out of the pen, Berton — who had been eyeing the terriers with great interest — went straight for the nearest one and, possibly suspecting it represented lunch, picked it up in his mouth. At that point, the terriers screamed, Haruko screamed, her mother screamed and her children screamed. Poor Berton. Horrified, he immediately dropped his "catch" and retreated, howling with terror, back into the pen. The terrier, of course, was totally uninjured, but still, Berton was the very picture of contrition. He had shamed himself — and us. He was mortified, and refused to leave the pen for the rest of that day, refused to eat his supper — and remained literally *hang-dog* all day Sunday.

I found his contrition very moving. He would not have harmed the dog — and didn't. Once it was in his mouth, he had known it wasn't lunch. He seemed humiliated by his mistake — as if he had done something unforgivable. Truth to tell, we were the ones who needed forgiving — for having allowed the encounter in the first place.

Our most recent pair of dogs are Casey and Minnie — an "almost" Border collie, an "almost" German shepherd — both rescued from the Beaverton animal shelter. They now have us so well trained that when we hear a certain high, tense tone in their barking, we know it is cold enough to move them into heated quarters.

Casey is, at heart, a dancer. He doesn't run; he prances. And as he goes, his white ruff swings from side to side in rhythm with his pace. It seems to signify his Scottish ancestry, just like a swaying kilt keeping time with a Highland fling. He is also a master at "tiptoeing over the horizon." There will be a casual toss of the head — *I'm just slipping down the field to inspect that tree* — and next thing we know, he's over at Len's place, visiting their dog, Tess.

Minnie, on the other hand, is totally down to earth. And to water. You always know when she is out of the pen, because the first thing you hear is a great *splat* as she belly-flops into the pond.

Each of them has a great smile and it's almost impossible not to return it in kind. I despair of anyone who maintains that animals have no emotions. Perhaps — as well as being blind and deaf — such people have no emotions themselves.

There has been, in all our relations with dogs, an uncomplicated but nonetheless wonderful communication regarding life and death. When Maggie's pups were being born in the back shed, for instance, she announced each arrival with a quick, sharp bark that said: *food, please.* Out we would go with warm milk, wait for her to drink and then retreat until the next birth.

Belle and Berton both told us when their deaths were due. Each — in that moment — refused to go back into the pen, and spent the remaining summer weeks at large, never straying from the garden. Berton, with a single look, informed us that his arthritic condition had become intolerable — and we called the vet. And Belle? One summer's day, she went to the truck, which we had always used to take her to the clinic, and she barked. *Now.* Of course, we complied, and off she went — for the final time. Into memory.

House Mice
and Church Mice

When does a farmhouse become a haven for mice? When the only indoor cat is old and blind, and twenty-seven vigorous mousers are living outside. This was our situation in the mid seventies, when the clatter of our typewriters was almost drowned out by the pitter-patter of tiny feet, palpitating across the ceilings and through the walls.

The house cat, then, was the unforgettable Mottle. The stonemason had found her one morning beside the driveway when he was finishing the pillars that marked its entrance. When he told us there was a thin, old cat out there, "behaving weird," we brought her into the house and settled her on one of the sofas. It happened that Bill had started cooking the breakfast bacon, and once the aroma reached the cat, she suddenly raised her head — and walked off the sofa into thin air. Which is to say, she behaved as if she was already on the floor. And that is how we discovered that she was blind.

She became the star of the place — in more ways than one. She was filmed for documentaries on perception and sleep;

she was adored by cats and people alike — and she was my constant companion, especially when I was playing the piano. She loved to sit beside me, her front paws resting near the keyboard, as she purred out her own vibrations to meet those she could apparently feel as well as hear.

Years later, after her death, I put her into one of my novels, *Not Wanted on the Voyage* — changing the spelling of her name to suit the biblical atmosphere of the story. She became Mottyl, one of the heroes of this retelling of the tale of Noah and the Ark.

As wonderful as she was, though, she was never the solution to our mouse problem.

Finally, I devised a non-lethal mousetrap: an old pyrex coffee pot, with a stepped arrangement of books to let the mice reach the pot's interior, where tempting bits of cheese awaited them. Once inside, they could not climb up the slippery pyrex. Perfect. Every morning I would tip-toe outside with a potful of well-fed mice and, having scouted the situation to make sure there were no cats skulking in wait nearby, I would release them onto the lawn. And, of course, every afternoon they would march back into the house and nap until it was time for me to set out their evening temptation.

After Mottle was gone, our indoor cats included a kitten, an ancient male and a middle-aged dedicated mouser. The pyrex coffee pot no longer needed emptying. No one was there.

Even then, the house wasn't completely mouse-free, and ultimately we came to recognize one of the survivors. Her left eye was scarred and closed — the result, we presumed, of some mishap in the past. Also, she was a creature of habit. Creeping onto the kitchen counter every morning, she would sit there on her haunches, unperturbed by our presence. While Bill and I ate our toast, she breakfasted on crumbs from the breadboard.

We called her Ingrid — remembering a story we'd heard

about Ingrid Bergman. While making the film *Notorious* with director Alfred Hitchcock, the Swedish actress had apparently arrived on the set early one morning more than a bit hung over. The day's first scene did not go well. Take after take after take. Finally, just before noon, Hitchcock was satisfied. He turned to Miss Bergman, smiled and said: *Good morning, Ingrid.* Which is what we said to our mouse.

One day Ingrid discovered a dog biscuit, forgotten on the counter. Bonanza! But much too heavy for one mouse to manage. After a bit of ineffective pushing and heaving, Ingrid scurried down behind the counter. We then heard a lot of excited mouse noise, and in minutes up she came with several of her offspring. Grunting in *Mouse,* they heaved the biscuit across the counter and tumbled it over the edge, after which the whole tiny family followed it like acrobats and had a joyous meal of smashed biscuit.

There was a period later on when the pantry was invaded, every night, by a mouse strong enough to knock things off the shelves — heavy things, such as canned food. Before long, we would hear the pantry mayhem during the day — large, empty jars and canisters suddenly pushed to the floor. Eventually, we caught a glimpse of him, scurrying across the open doorway between kitchen and pantry. He was certainly large — and very dark. Perhaps an oversized and energetic meadow vole. As we pondered the problem of what to do about him, we began referring to him as Godzilla.

Before any solution had been achieved to the problem of this "supermouse," we had to be away for several weeks; a new novel was being published, and that meant a national promotional tour. When we finally got back, one of the first questions we asked Len Collins was: "what about Godzilla?"

Len's face was a study in mixed emotions, but all he said was: "he's gone."

My first thought, which I voiced, was: "I hope you didn't use a trap!"

The answer was in the negative — but the explanation was so embarrassing that we never did get around to finding out just what solved the problem of Godzilla. And the *real* problem, of course, turned out that he was not a mouse. He was a rat. In fact, Godzilla was a whole *family* of rats.

May they rest in peace. Certainly, now that they're gone, the pantry does.

After that, our rodent problems were few. It was simply a matter of adapting. We found, for example, that if we kept the bird-feeder seed in metal bins, the mice no longer chewed through the plastic bags in which the feed arrived, but were content simply to clean up the minor spillages that occurred when the teenagers were restocking the feeders. A series of canisters for flour, crackers and cookies kept mouse depredations to a minimum, although absolutely nothing ever seemed to keep the teenagers from the cookies. At least, we think it was the teenagers. Mice, I think, do not know how to reseal bags of Mister Christie's Oreos.

There was one mouse who, a few years later, used to make regular visits to the dishwasher. Before the rinse cycle, there was usually something delectable clinging to the plates. We decided that the visitor wasn't much of a nuisance, and that we could all learn to live together. And what *we* had to learn was: before starting the washer, make sure the mouse wasn't in there.

One winter day, Bill forgot. He had been at the typewriter, trying to meet a deadline, was being constantly interrupted by phone calls and still had some kitchen chores to finish — including the breakfast dishes. Just as he was putting detergent into the washer, the doorbell rang. He looked out the kitchen window and gritted his teeth. It was two nervous members of a local, highly evangelical Christian church, still persisting in their attempts to convert us to their beliefs. Snow-pale faces and quivering pamphlets. We thought of them as "the Church Mice." Bracing himself to be polite, Bill headed out to meet them, absent-mindedly closing the washer and turning it on as he passed.

Just as he opened the front door, he remembered. "Oh, God," he said, "I forgot the mouse!" and dashed back to the dishwasher, opening it to discover the terrified creature — soaked, but otherwise unharmed. He quickly picked it up and wrapped it gently in a tea-towel. "I'll be right with you," he called out. "I'm just drying the mouse!"

By the time Bill had released it and got back to the door, the Church Mice — now in a state of nervous collapse — had gone. Obviously, the inhabitants of Stone Orchard were beyond redemption.

Flights of Angels

The first of our Stone Orchard dogs died in 1973. Her name
was Maggie; never to be forgotten. We brought her up from
the Toronto Humane Society, where she had been condemned
to die because no one had claimed her. One of the vets, having
overheard that we lived in the country, begged us to take her.
The man had tears in his eyes. *Please,* he said. *Her life has
been hell.* She was watching us. I looked at her.

She came to Stone Orchard that afternoon. More than
thirty years ago.

Her life *had* been hell. A street dog, eating from garbage
cans, sleeping in the rain. Now, at home, jumping down from
the car, she could see the wide fields and the wider sky and she
began to run in huge, cantering circles, barking — virtually
crying out with joy.

About nine years later, she had a series of strokes and we
had to take her out for her walks in a wheelbarrow. She
adored this. We called her the Empress of China. When she
died, I claimed the privilege of digging her grave. We buried
her beneath an apple tree in whose shade she had often lain
and as I dug, with Maggie lying beside me on an old blue
towel, a bird came and sat in the branches above us and sang

and sang and sang. Looking up, I saw that it was a rose-breasted grosbeak, a bird we had never seen here before and have not seen since. Once and once only. That day.

This was the first of what can only be called "bird phenomena" — a sequence of extraordinary and inexplicable bird appearances that seemed to be connected to death.

Birds, of course, are pretty phenomenal in and of themselves. Nothing declares spring more profoundly than the morning songs of robins or the evening cries of foraging killdeer. Equally, the coming of the autumn is proclaimed by growing hosts of sparrows, chickadees and bluejays. Augmented by other winter visitors — one year, more than one hundred evening grosbeaks — they begin what amounts to a siege that will last until spring.

Still, some species have all but disappeared — thanks to the indiscriminate use of pesticides. Birds that once came here in flocks of twenty — forty — sixty — stopped arriving altogether: meadow larks, martins, swallows, bobolinks, flycatchers, snipe, flickers, cuckoos, thrashers and some woodpeckers. The fault was not entirely with county spraying — it also lay in the American south, where most of these birds overwinter. DDT was especially lethal. The birds, ingesting a diet of increasingly chemical-laden insects, became sterile. We watched for three years in a row as the martins in Len Collins's martin house failed to produce young. That was when they disappeared — and have never reappeared.

Happily, now that wisdom has prevailed — or, at least, begun to prevail — the bobolinks, woodpeckers and swallows are beginning to make a comeback. Last year, I saw one meadow lark, two phoebes and three crested flycatchers. A beginning.

Most of the winter visitors still come in great numbers. I don't know who profits most from this immense influx — whether it's the birds, the seed merchants or Bill and me. Three hundred pounds of peanuts in the shell ring a joyful bell on the cash register, but at the same time, I get to know my name in jay-ese: a wild raucous cheer not unlike the shouts that greet a goal scored in hockey. *Here comes the peanut man!* That's me.

In the pantry, we mix up great pots of millet, niger and small sunflower seeds for the finches, sparrows and redpolls. Their feeder hangs from a tree outside the kitchen window, and near it, suet is set out for the woodpeckers — in a container provided by one of the lads who worked here. Above the suet-rack, there is a leering, painted cat waiting to pounce. So far, it has not deterred a single bird — only the other cats, who — in spite of our own discouragements — used to climb the tree to take their turn as non-successful hunters at the feeding station.

This brings to mind my fury — and my bafflement — at the number of people who actively drive off such fellow feeders at the station as squirrels, raccoons, and starlings. Raccoons, these people say, are "greedy" and "messy," squirrels are "thieves," starlings aren't "pretty." Where did this élitism come from? If we choose to feed wildlife, we choose to feed wildlife — not just "the chosen few."

A few years ago, we noticed five or six starlings in the dog pen, picking up bits of leftover kibble. Now, we scatter dog kibble down by the pond, and find ourselves feeding numbers that have finally stabilized, and that come, whatever the weather, every winter day: more than ninety starlings and, year after year, three faithful crows.

Equally faithful are the Canada geese — not just to this place, but to each other. The same pair returned for years to nest on the small island in the centre of our pond. We could easily recognize them: the gander had an uncharacteristic white spot on the black of his head, and the goose had a slightly withered foot. We never found out whether it was the result of an infection, or of an encounter with one of the leg-hold traps that sadly are still set out along the river and in our local marshes.

I considered trying to catch her in order to have her examined by the vets, and I mentioned this one day to a visitor, John Livingston, of the world's leading naturalists. John took me to task, telling me that it was one thing to help save natural habitats, but quite another to meddle with the lives of individual creatures. Basically, he pointed out that sharing the planet means respecting and being a part of natural balances — not interfering with them. And to act to prolong the life of "our" injured goose would be just that — interference. This did not mean, he added, that we cannot come to the aid of an animal in immediate distress.

I appreciated his point, but it didn't make me feel any better when, the following spring, the gander appeared — alone. We never saw the goose again. And all that summer, the gander spent most of his time alone, apparently disconsolate, on the island or in the water beside it.

The *next* year, however, there *were* two geese on the pond — and the gander had the unmistakeable white mark on his head. He had found a new mate — and they raised six goslings that year. My first reaction was utter joy. My second? That perhaps, after all, John was right. The geese have been back every year since. Nature's balance had prevailed.

When Maggie died and the rose-breasted grosbeak sang in the apple tree, it was only the first of many such inexplicable visitations. While I was burying her son Hooker, a few years later, a flock of Canada geese flew over his grave — wheeled, came back and made a second pass. More recently, the night we had to put down our beloved malamute, Berton, a great horned owl came and sat above his burial place.

Lastly, when Bill's mother died in 1983, we scattered her

ashes in our garden. Suddenly, without a word, Bill pulled at my arm. Standing in the field just beyond the fence below the pond was a solitary sandhill crane. Why was it there? What did it mean? I cannot say. What I can say is that sandhill cranes are western birds — and Bill's mother hailed from Regina.

Somehow, this doesn't seem to call for understanding. Acceptance will do.

Aquatic Adventures

WATER MAY BE FRIEND OR FOE; IT COMES AND GOES too little or too much; getting rid of it may be as hard as waiting for its arrival in the first place — but whatever water's problems, nothing can live without it.

Water Hazards

It is now more than thirty years since Bill and I came to Stone Orchard — city-born and city-bred innocents, unversed in the skills of country living. Certainly unversed in the mysteries of country water.

We found that the kitchen taps delivered a good strong flow of the stuff and although it was clear enough, the taste and the smell were terrible. The flavour was finally explained by the electrician who had come in the meanwhile to do some essential reworking of our home's ancient wiring. He watched in horror as Bill filled a glass at the sink one hot September day — and drank it down. We had experienced enough of our electrician's habits to suspect that water was not his favourite beverage. Still, his reaction seemed a bit extreme.

"You're *drinking* that?" he said.

Bill smiled and dried the glass. "Of course. Why not?"

"But that's not drinking water. You get that out in the back shed from the pump. There's a well there."

We'd certainly noticed the hand pump in the shed, but had assumed it was a back-up if a storm cut off our electricity and paralyzed our pressure system. We weren't total idiots. Or so we had thought.

The electrician tried again.

"Have you cleaned the cistern?"

Cistern? What cistern?

"In the basement. I had to work around it last time I checked the wiring. But that was five years ago. The house has been empty since then. The cistern is bound to need some refreshing."

Refreshing, we thought, was an interesting choice of words. Perhaps he meant we could modify the stench coming from the taps. So we put on our rubber boots and went down into the basement. Sure enough, there was the cistern: a high-walled oblong cement structure into which we peered with the help of flashlights. And there, floating on the water or dimly seen beneath its surface were a groundhog corpse, two rat corpses and a decomposed squirrel. At that moment, we lost our citi-fied innocence. Also our appetite. Also — nearly — our lunch.

After we had removed and buried the dead, we poured in a gallon of chlorine and closed the cellar door. We didn't bathe for more than a week, and we started pumping our drinking and cooking water by hand out in the shed. In the meantime, having had the well tested, we knew it was grade-A quality water — hard, but tasty, refreshing and safe.

We depended on the cistern and the old, hand-dug well for fifteen years. Sometimes, in winter, we had to melt the ice in the pump and its pipes, and we always kept two or three extra pails of water standing by. I was reminded of a woman Bill and I had met in the Northwest Territories south of Fort Smith. She had told us that her main occupation in the depths of winter and minus forty-degree temperatures was melting snow on her wood stove, there being no electricity. Every pot of water required six to eight times its capacity in snow. At least Bill and I didn't have to do that. Finally, we were able to afford to have a motorized unit come in and drill a well deep enough to supply all our water needs. In fact, we ultimately drilled two of them — the second well to act as back-up, and also to fill the swimming pool.

For those first fifteen years, however, our water system continued to provide a series of adventures.

The cistern remained a hazard — not for us, but for the cats. Until we built the first "new wing," they could enter the basement through the back shed that housed the old well. And if, for any reason, they couldn't find drinking water outside, they would seek out the cistern. We were unaware of this until the day we heard frantic splashing in the basement. One of the older cats — Moth — had fallen in. We immediately fished her out — and it's hard to say which of the three of us was most terrified by the experience. We wrapped her in a towel and took her outside to dry off in the sun. And then we went back into the basement to create a cat-saving device. It consisted of a length of window-screening fixed to the top of the cistern and extending down into the water. There was no need to test it, as we had already been using the same system in the swimming pool outside — and had seen it work with kittens, squirrels and frogs.

The former owners had tacked sheets of galvanized tin all around the pump in the shed to keep dirt from falling through the cracks between the floorboards and possibly contaminating the well. For this we were grateful — until the night I went downstairs in my nightshirt to pump myself a carafe of water for beside the bed.

As I pumped, I glanced out through the open door into the moonlit yard. What a glorious night it was — at the height of Indian summer. And there was Max, the largest of our seven cats, trotting across the yard. He was carrying something in his mouth. Max always shared the triumphs of the hunt with me. This time, the gift he dropped at my feet was a rat. *Thank you.*

This rat was still very much in control of his destiny. Panic-stricken, he glanced around for a quick escape route. There was my nightshirt, hanging low above his head. With one nimble bound, he began to crawl up the inside of the garment. The beat of my feet on the metal sheets plus the wailing sounds that issued from my throat were enough to galvanize the animals, let alone the tin. The poor rat dropped down and disappeared out the door, followed by Max, the cat — not in pursuit, but in flight.

Shortly afterwards, Max moved into the village. I like to think it was not our misadventure with the rat that prompted his decision, but the fact that our cat population was growing so quickly. Max and his sister, Mouse, had been our original pair. Now, it was possible there were too many others for the founder of the clan to cope with.

Whatever the reason, we later discovered that big Max had taken up with an ex-wrestler and his family — and there he lived out the rest of his life, contented and secure.

Meanwhile, we continued to cope with all the problems involved with pets — and plumbing.

Our most disastrous plumbing adventure occurred years later, just after Bill and I had returned from a lengthy tour for one of my books. We were enjoying the new wing Len Collins had completed for us just before the tour. At any moment, the doorbell would announce the arrival of our traditional New Year's house guests. Watering some house plants, I noticed an aroma drifting in from the new wing's ground floor — the studio. *My, it certainly is ripe in there!*

The source of the aroma was soon discovered. In our absence, a crucial pipe-fitting — one of the new ones — had come undone in the walls, pouring two-months' worth of sewage not into the septic tank, but into the crawl space beneath the studio. As always, it was Len to the rescue, sump pump and industrial vacuum in hand and with new pipe-fitting to be installed. And thank heaven for his sense of humour. Two hours later, one of the house guests momentarily forgot what was going on and automatically flushed a toilet just as Len was about to join up the open ends of the pipe . . .

Here, I would like to point out the prime rule in moving to the country: choose a property across the road from Len Collins. This way, you will survive.

Yes, country living has its water hazards, but they tend to fade to insignificance in the face of aqueous benefits: the taste of rock-cold well water, clear and fresh from the ground, now delivered through our taps; the liquid mirror of the pond in its field; the summer sound of rain running into the cistern, from which we run the hose that waters the garden, and the smell of it in the barrels set beneath the downspouts from the eaves — the scent of mint and cedar, oak staves and moss.

Day in, day out, we bless the blissful ignorance that allowed us to take up residence at Stone Orchard thirty years ago. But for that ignorance, we would not have any of the joys of country living — including the laughter that is our daily companion as we wonder what will happen next.

How I Tried
to Save the World

Think globally, act locally. That's one way — I've been told
— to save the world. And so, back in the 1970s, I launched a
one-man campaign — not to save the whole world, but to
help save a very small part of it: our local population of
beaver and muskrat.

We live near the Beaver River, which flows through
Cannington on its way to Lake Simcoe. It's safe to assume, I
think, that it was named for the animal that was once
commonly seen in and around it — and that is also one of the
symbols of our nation. What's common today, however, is not
the beaver, but the irony of the river's name. In the same ironic
vein, have you ever noticed that almost every new "development" is named for what was destroyed in order to create it?
Maple Glen — with not a maple tree left in sight. *Pine Ridge*
— where both the pines and the ridge have been eradicated to
clear and level new building sites.

As Jimmy Durante used to growl in so many of his films:
what a revoltin' development!

Anyway . . . back to the beaver; to those still remaining in our local wetlands. They were considered a nuisance. Their dams got in the way along "our" river; they felled "our" trees. They — along with the muskrat — were also seen as a source of profit. Both species were being threatened not only through loss of habitat, but because there was still a fur trade — and thus, there was trapping.

I made a decision. Single-handedly, I would wage war against that instrument of torture, the leg-hold trap.

I had a very simple strategy, and I put it into action. I went into Cannington and bought every leg-hold trap offered for sale by the local hardware store. Thirty-five of them. There. Done.

A week later, the stock had been replenished. Again, I bought every one. And next week — they were back. The light dawned. This is not working, Tiff. Sadly, the trapping went on until our beavers and muskrats have pretty well disappeared. That didn't do much to save the world.

Think globally, act locally. I sat out on the back lawn and thought globally. What was it that was threatening the world — degrading the environment, wiping out species after species? Attitude. We have the wrong attitude. We think because we have the ability, we also have the *right* to do whatever we want with the rest of nature. And we keep getting it *wrong*. So I went upstairs to my study and started to write a book.

I set it here, on this farm. One of its heroines was our blind cat — called Mottyl, in the book. It was another version of Noah and the Ark — *Not Wanted on the Voyage* — an allegory about a strong-willed man who lost touch with his God, and so decided to make up his own rules and say that God had given them to him. And that, in this book, is how we gained "dominion over nature" — we gave it to ourselves, claiming that our right to it came from God. Well — the book hasn't saved the world. But I'm proud to say it has altered a few attitudes, my own included.

While I was upstairs, beginning that book, Bill was down at the kitchen table, mapping out a television series with our neighbour and old friend, John Livingston — the environmentalist with whom Bill had worked on the CBC television series "The Nature of Things." The new programs were ultimately presented under the title "A Planet for the Taking." They, too, dealt with the attitude that was robbing the world of its natural variety, vigour and balances; in other words, of its ability to survive. Tragically, that attitude still persists — the one that sees present profits more valuable than future survival. Still, no matter how many battles are lost, the war against this attitude cannot be abandoned.

THINK GLOBALLY, ACT LOCALLY. Spring, summer and fall, Bill and I often took the kayak out on the Beaver River, which flows beneath the bridge just down the road. In some winters, whenever the winds blew the frozen surface clear of snow, we could skate for miles down its winding course. The rest of the year it's heaven-sent in other ways — a river whose peepers sing to us every spring night, a river with green and leopard frogs sitting on lily pads, kingfishers plunging from overhanging branches, darting swallows skimming its waters, great blue herons prospecting the shallows, while painted turtles bask on half-submerged deadwood and snapping turtles rest on its muddy banks. Heading south, this meandering waterway broadens into a wide, lush stretch of marshland where you can drift amongst the reeds and listen to the redwings. An aquatic paradise, with only one sign of human presence — an abandoned railway track, where trains used to skirt the marsh and follow the river-line north.

We used to walk nine miles along that track every winter. It was our "beat" in the annual Christmas bird count. I would urge anyone to join that count, sometime. Give yourself the pleasure.

Some years ago, the trains stopped running up through Cannington and beyond, and the track was finally torn up. Abandoned, I thought. A passage no longer used by train, but used by animals — human and otherwise. *Save it.* But how? There's that same old attitude: *Frogs, turtles and birds, Findley? What use are they? Bullrushes, Findley? More like plain bull.* Except — and we know this now — it isn't bull. It's a scientific fact. When the frogs, turtles, birds and bullrushes are gone, we will go next. Destroy their habitat — and we ultimately destroy our own.

Well, I went home and phoned some friends who lived in or near Cannington — people who knew as much as anyone could about ecology and about the municipal structure and politics of our area. John Livingston, Arthur and Alice Boissonneau, Susan Lillico Lewis. Together, we pondered the future of our river, its marshes and its creatures. Could there be a wetlands sanctuary?

Think globally — act locally. We got in touch with the Lake Simcoe Region Conservation Authority. It turned out they were already interested in the unused right of way where the trains had run. Make it practical, they told us. Don't talk frogs, talk money. Tax benefits, tourism, jobs.

Susan — the expert in local government resources — helped us get the name of every landowner along that stretch of the river. We wrote letters, held meetings, answered questions, sought out whatever answers we didn't already know. We wrote more letters. Eventually, the Conservation Authority managed to raise enough money to buy the right of way.

Later, we were present when the Beaver River Nature Trail was opened — the first active step in preserving the Beaver and its marshes. It was then we retired from the project, since the Conservation Authority had taken on the long-term business of trying to acquire the rest of the land along the river — land, by the way, too wet for farming and, we have prayed, too impractical for industrial development.

Then came Mister Harris's Ontario budget cuts and his anti-conservation bill. In a word, our Conservation Authorities themselves may now be an endangered species.

Wouldn't it be wonderful if I could just nip into town and buy them all up. That way, week by week, they would reappear. If only.

Drought

When we came to live at Stone Orchard, a white wire fence formed the boundary between the front yard and the road, running from one end of the house lot to the other. This fence was not at all unattractive. It had ornate loops and picturesque gates and it was set in concrete. It was sturdy and during cattle drives, it kept the cows from coming in and helping themselves to our lawn — not to mention our day lilies. The only problem was, the openwork fence provided no privacy. So — and here the story takes on the first of its ironic twists — we took it out.

We had help, of course. The concrete foundation was two feet deep and a back-hoe had to come and break it up so it could be carted away to the dump. A neighbour took the fence itself for his own front yard, muttering *perfect* under his breath. It's still there.

Our thought had been — and here we go again — *we will plant a cedar hedge*. Attractive — practical — relatively fast-growing . . . simple. Hah! God knows how many young trees we planted. Certainly a good deal more than a hundred. *Won't they be spectacular, all trimmed up and six feet tall! Don't they smell wonderful!* And then — *what do you mean they have to be watered twice a day?*

Only for the first week, our advisory literature informed us. After that — *once a day will be ample.*

Oh.

Here is where I have to tell you that our cistern held only a thousand gallons and the well for drinking water was only fifteen feet deep and produced an average of less than a gallon a minute. Four is acceptable. From five to six is perfect.

There were only two of us. Outside, there was no pressure system and therefore no hose — only four pails. We filled them at the kitchen sink and ran the cistern dry in two days. Then — we had a drought. One whole month — and no rain.

We bought water — having it trucked in to fill the cistern. We carried the pails. I think we even carried them in our sleep. And all this while, the cedars faded before our eyes. Faded and died. The well water was too cold — and anyway, the well ran dry. Neighbours with a deeper well than ours kindly supplied us with huge bottles of drinking water. We prayed for rain, but the rain god was busy elsewhere.

Bill is from Regina. The prairies. In his childhood, he had witnessed the dustbowl effects of the 1930s — the land and the cattle dying — people forced from their farms. The worst that can happen. Our little dying trees were nothing, by comparison. At least we didn't have livestock. Still, *why won't it rain?* became the cry of the day.

In time, of course, it did rain. But it was too late. The cedar hedge was dead. I kept watching it, making rain prayers even as it poured. *More! More! More!* But the hedge did not revive. We pulled it out and ploughed it under. For five years, we sat and stared, and listened to the road. And the road rolled on by, so it seemed, as it stared, and listened to us.

Then, a charming young man came by, selling young trees. His charming prices were affordable; his charming descriptions of their rapid growth and their hardiness were irresistible. *They can practically survive on air alone!* he told us. We almost emptied the bank account to buy a hundred of them — sugar maples, just like the ancient giants that stood in a row between the west lawn and the road. Again, and this time with help, we planted them — not only across the front of the house lot, but along the northern boundary of the entire farm. We would have the finest display of sugar maples in the whole area! How charming! And how ill-fated.

We immediately had another drought. And an entire tree line of dead young maples. I'm happy to add that the ancient giants survived. Their roots ran deep enough to save them.

In later years we had to save those same huge trees from another threat — an ironic twist on the subject of water shortages. Remember all those calls for rain? Well, by the 1980s, we were getting plenty of rain. Acid rain, thanks to the sulphur dioxide pouring into the atmosphere from the industrial smokestacks to the south of us. And all the maples along our road — in fact, in the whole area — were beginning to turn yellow and drop their leaves — in July. Having already lost almost all our elms to the plague of Dutch elm disease, we were frantic and frustrated as we watched a number of our maples wither and begin to die.

Then, by chance, we came across an article about a small firm in Ontario that had made a remarkable discovery. In developing an effective fertilizer for golf greens, they had found that on courses treated with their product, the maple trees nearest the greens were flourishing — while those in the surrounding fields and woods were beginning to die back.

Bill immediately got in touch with them, pinpointed their location near Elmira, drove there and filled the car with dozens of sacks of the miracle fertilizer. In fact, he bought up almost the whole of their remaining stock. It's a good thing he did, because what he'd found when he got to Elmira was a young company going out of business. Nobody seemed willing to say just why. They had been making a modest profit, but Dow and other chemical manufacturers seemed to have claimed the field. And the golf greens.

At any rate, we stored the sacks in the drive-shed, and set about applying some of the contents to the biggest maples out front. Our method was simple. Using a crowbar, we drove multiple holes in the lawn, in a pattern governed by the farthest reach of each tree's branches. The holes were about one-third of a metre deep; we poured in fertilizer up to the three-quarter level. We thought at first that topping the holes with bits of turf would finish the job — but we didn't reckon with the raccoons, or with their apparent taste for this substance. They kept uncovering the holes and emptying them. Finally, we learned to place a thick stone beneath each turf-plug and this brought success.

So, apparently, did the fertilizer. We have used it every year since — on the maples and on the weeping willows around the pond. And while maples along the rest of the roadside have all but disappeared, our treated trees are still flourishing.

There is no end of reasons to go on persuading polluting industries to stop creating acid rain, but until the battle is won at last, it's good to know there is at least one effective protection against a part of the onslaught.

All the while — until a high stone wall solved the problem of privacy — we went back to watching the traffic along the road and in the field on the other side. One day during yet another drought, we were at lunch, gazing out the window at the sweltering landscape. We saw two cats strolling across the meadow, heading towards the house. We immediately recognized the one in the lead; it was Moth, who revelled in the mousing opportunities of the wilds. But we couldn't make out which cat was following her. Perhaps a new one. Its legs were shorter than most cats', which meant that keeping pace with Moth was something of a problem. Soon enough we saw the reason for this. As the two started across the road towards Stone Orchard, we realized that the second animal was not a cat — but a groundhog.

After the strolling pair had disappeared around the side of the house, we rose from the table to look out the back screen door where, on the porch, there was one of the cats' many water bowls. And drinking from it was Moth — while the groundhog sat on its haunches, watching. In a moment, Moth looked up, turned away and sat washing her face as the groundhog took its turn at the water bowl. We had to wonder what kind of language had bridged the species gap to bring about this unique form of sharing. And it continued throughout the summer. The groundhog appeared there many times and though we worried about its safe passage on the road, it made it all the way to its winter hibernation under the field. Perhaps it dreamt, down there, of sunny days and water bowls.

Take Two Cups of Snow

Lengthening days are a welcome sign of spring after a particularly stiff dose of winter. Still, a blanket of snow is part of our national heritage and a symbol of our endurance. It flavours our experience of being Canadian. When the fields of white that surround Stone Orchard are marked off with split-rail fences and barren trees that might have been drawn by charcoal, we seem to be living inside a painting by David Milne or Clarence Gagnon.

Nowadays, the white may still be pure — but not the snow. The same chemicals that produce acid rain now pollute winter precipitation as well. If you have, as we do, any old recipes that call for "pure, fresh snow" — you're in trouble.

Winter is still beautiful — and still demanding. Fortunately, Len Collins now ploughs the driveway we used to shovel out by hand, while teenage workers take on other chores — clearing paths out to the dog-pen and down to the frozen pond, where we scatter extra dog kibble for our resident starlings and crows; hauling in several hundred pounds of various seeds and peanuts to stock the hanging bird feeders; endlessly filling the wheelbarrow with firewood to feed the fireplaces and the greenhouse stove. When temperatures plummet, we move the outdoor cats into the greenhouse, while the dogs spend their nights on straw piled into the partly heated cat shed. With dogs especially, it is essential to keep them out of the wind, and all domestic pets should be given extra shelter if the temperature drops to minus twenty-two degrees Celsius.

Near-record snowfalls in the sixties and seventies made our first winters here a time of hazardous driving. That was when Bill and I were both working in radio and television, and commuting to Toronto several days a week. The journey home was always in the dark and often through a blinding blizzard. Back then, we drove a Citroën, whose hydraulic suspension system would give the car invaluable added clearance. That allowed us to blast our way through the soft drifts that built up as soon as the snowploughs had passed. It was slow going, but we could always make it up the highway, into Cannington and out to our own sideroad. There, we might have to stop. Since that was as far as the ploughs went at night, our road remained completely plugged till morning by deep, wind-packed snow.

At the corner I would get out in order to help guide Bill as he carefully edged the Citroën into the ditch — just far enough to keep it from being hit during the next day's ploughing. Overnight, given the prevailing northwest wind, the car might be completely drifted over. Knowing that Leonard Griffin would ultimately use his team of horses to haul our abandoned vehicle back onto the road, we would then flounder home through two hundred yards of thigh-deep snow.

One friend, Beverley Roberts, made it all the way from Montreal through a raging snowstorm, only to be blocked at the same corner. Bill was by then an expert at ditching cars, so he manoeuvred Beverley's Chevy into place and we began the several journeys required to unload it. Since it was Christmas, there were gifts to be brought in. Also suitcases, extra coats and a box of wine in danger of freezing. One of the gifts was special — a dozen croissants from Aux Délices, our favourite Montreal restaurant and bakery — now, I'm sorry to say, no longer there.

Returning to the house with our final armfuls, we found the box from Aux Délices on the floor. Empty. Oh, damn! We had forgotten the dogs had been brought in out of the cold. Clearly, they approved of what Beverley had brought from Montreal. Not a crumb remained. Lying by the fire, Maggie and Hooker were indulging in licking what remained of their buttery feast from their paws and chops. They were so contented, we could do nothing but laugh.

The next morning, however, we still managed a special breakfast treat — one we used to enjoy every winter. It's a pioneer concoction, quintessentially Canadian, since one of its two ingredients is freshly fallen snow — pure snow, a rare commodity these days. Even now, though — if we're lucky — some late snowfall may be preceded by enough spring rain to rinse the air of most of its unwanted chemicals. Then — to the kitchen.

Mix four or five parts of snow — depending on how fluffy it is — and one part of cornmeal. Place the mixture in greased muffin pans — we use bacon fat, for flavour — and bake for fifteen minutes at 425°F. As the melting snow provides liquid, the natural gases gathered by the falling flakes are released by heat and bubble out to provide leavening. Serve this "snow-bread" with lots of butter and maple syrup. Not Aux Délices, but still delicious.

If you want to carry some sense of winter into the rest of the year, try making your own ice cream. At Stone Orchard, we've always done it in the traditional way, with an old-fashioned freezer in which you embed a container in cracked ice and salt, then crank the handle to stir the creamy contents while they're freezing.

We've also prepared ice cream in the French style — using egg yolks, which leaves us enough whites to also have a freshly baked angel food cake, topped with Sea Foam icing. More about that later.

Our freezer produced about four quarts of ice cream at a time — so here's how we made it:

Heat gently until steaming 4 cups of milk. Stir in 2 cups sugar and 1/2 tsp. salt.

Grate 6 oz. unsweetened chocolate and set aside.

Mix 1 cup of sugar with 1 cup of cocoa, then slowly add, while stirring, 1/2 cup of milk. Add grated chocolate last. Mix well.

Separate yolks and whites of 12 eggs — keeping 2 whites apart from the other 10. Beat the yolks, then pour part of the heated milk mixture over them, beat well and return yolk mixture to the rest of the heated milk. Stir and cook (without boiling) until this custard thickens. Add the chocolate mixture, stir well again, then chill. At this point, you can hold the mixture in the refrigerator until you are ready to make the ice cream.

Prepare 2 cups of sliced almonds by cooking them carefully in a frying pan with 3 tbsp. of butter; when they are browned, drain them on paper towels and set aside.

When you are ready to complete the ice cream:

Add to the chocolate cream: 3 tbsp. vanilla and 6 cups of chilled, unbeaten whipping cream, and stir well.

Prepare the freezer: pour the chocolate cream mixture into the container and set it in place inside the bucket. (Our bucket is wooden.) Pack cracked ice (pieces about one-quarter the size of an ice-cube) around the container, tamping the ice down with a hammer handle, until the freezer is almost half full. Then alternate layers of ice with layers of pickling salt, using up to 2 cups of salt. Put crank assembly onto the freezer and add enough ice to cover the container.

Crank slowly until you feel the contents begin to congeal. Carefully take off the lid of the container and add the browned almonds. Replace the lid and crank as quickly as you can until it's almost impossible to turn the handle.

You now have three choices: you can serve the ice cream immediately; you can take out the beaters and, leaving the container in position — place waxed paper or foil over the top of the container before replacing the lid, then top up the ice and salt in the freezer, cover the whole thing with sacking or carpeting and set aside until later; or you can scrape the still-soft ice cream into smaller containers and put them in the freezer compartment of your refrigerator for later use.

As for the angel food cake — use up to 10 of the whites in whatever recipe you like, then ice the cooled cake with Seven-Minute Sea Foam Icing whose recipe will be found in Bill's favourite all-purpose cook book: Irma Rombauer's *Joy of Cooking:*

Use an electric beater to combine, in the top of a double boiler: 2 egg whites, 1½ cups firmly packed brown sugar, ⅛ tsp. salt, 5 tbsp. water. Place over boiling water and beat for 5 minutes. Remove double boiler from heat, and continue beating —

still over the hot water — for 2 minutes. Place the top container in cold water and beat for a final 3 minutes. Add 1 tsp. vanilla and spread over the top and sides of the cake.

Finally, melt 2 cubes of unsweetened chocolate and dribble it across the top, letting it run down the sides. You can, if you like, swirl the icing with a fork to get a marbled effect.

Serve the cake with your homemade chocolate almond ice cream — and enjoy them as much as we always did at Stone Orchard. Your arms might still be aching from all that cranking, but there's always strength enough remaining to lift a spoon.

Waterworks

"We're going to have a real pond," Bill said. "Now."

We were out beyond the fence south of the garden. Our old pond lay behind us in a circle of willow trees and rushes. It was about the size of an average swimming pool — a shallow replica of the prairie dugouts of Bill's Saskatchewan childhood. Every spring it filled to overflowing and through each summer its waters would slowly evaporate until, by autumn, there would only be a pittance left. What's more, recent years had produced a series of droughts, some of which had left the dugout nothing but a pit lined with dried, sun-cracked mud.

We had promised ourselves that the last major project at Stone Orchard would be a large, self-sustaining pond. This promise, first made in 1964, had been renewed so often that it had taken on the character of a New Year's resolution: *a promise made to be broken.*

For more than twenty-five years I had dreamed about this pond, this water. Waking on summer mornings, I imagined it out beyond the spruce and willow trees, its shimmering surface already a part of the landscape — its wetness a haven to all kinds of creatures. But all I could see, in reality, was the muddy hollow we had, for years, tried to make into "our pond."

As if it were a desert mirage, the dream pond refused to let go of our imaginations. Water is intrinsically part of human life — of who and what we are. The sight of it — the taste of it — the feel of it — even the thought of it is life sustaining. The fact is, the earth's great oceans are the amniotic fluid of the entire human race and all else that lives. Sinking into it — seemingly weightless — gives an almost immediate sense of peace and well-being. It is not for nothing that for centuries, baths have been used to tranquillize the sick and pacify the mad.

Now, in spite of the continuing drought, Bill, the scientist, was making this bold declaration: the time had finally come to have our own body of lasting water. And although I've always had faith in Bill's fund of scientific knowledge, I was more than a little alarmed when he said we would go for a depth of six metres and a width of almost forty. By the old count, in which I still dream, this would be twenty feet deep and more than a hundred feet wide!

"How will we fill it?" I asked, trying not to sound too sceptical.

"You'll see," he said.

Oh, sure. *If you dig it, the water will come . . .*

An excavator, two trucks and a back-hoe rolled into the field one October morning and the digging began. The pond was to be shaped like the letter Q — with a small island in the middle and the old dugout forming a shallow "tail." Two weeks later, we had a crater in our field. Huge — and empty.

All winter long, the dogs and I made forays into its depths. At six metres, the excavators had expected to strike water. But the drought had lowered the water table beyond their reach. And ours. Instead, the autumn rains and snow had made a quagmire at the bottom and the island, with its willow and cedar trees, stuck up out of the hole like some landscape gardener's mistake — an aberration.

Eventually, the spring run-off began — at first, barely a trickle. I said nothing — even though, at this rate, it would take at least three years to fill the pond. Bill just said: *be patient* and gave his maddeningly self-confident smile. Then, one night, the temperature rose and it began to rain. I was awakened by a sound that up until that moment I had heard only in dreams. It was the sound of rushing, pounding water — all the taps of heaven seemingly opened by some mad angel thinking the time had come for the Second Flood.

We went out with flashlights into the rain to see what was happening. *Niagara.*

A virtual torrent of water was gushing from the culvert that drained the fields to the east and was cascading down into the crater. Its great hollow was already almost half-filled. Within another day — as the spring melt continued — the pond was overflowing where Bill had created a buried run-off culvert and the excavators had made a dip in the banks. The culvert spilled its water along a streaming crease in the land, heading westward towards the Beaver River — pausing it so happened, at the Khokar farm next door to fill their pond. It seemed a miracle. Two ponds, not one, and ours a dream that had finally come true.

What's more, the miracle has persisted. The run-off stream dries up before the end of May, but now the pond itself, thanks to its six-metre depth, holds enough water to withstand evaporation and maintain good levels even through the hottest summer months. Moreover, having witnessed its minimal loss of water, we believe there is seepage from the old springs, now the water table has been revived.

Early April, the pond is pregnant with ten thousand lives — with frogs and toads and snails; with crayfish, water striders, water boatmen and mayfly larvae; with algae, plants and grasses and other botanical organisms I cannot name. It is a magnet to everything living. The deer come up from the woods at dusk and dawn; the foxes arrive after dark. Raccoons and rabbits leave their tracks. Geese, ducks, herons return each year and kingfishers, swallows and killdeer skim its surface.

All the pond lacked was fish. We decided on the most elegant and colourful fish we knew — koi, the Japanese carp. Twenty-four fingerlings from a nearby aquatic nursery were introduced. Black and gold and silver, white and yellow and red. Added to these were sixteen goldfish, donated by a friend whose own small backyard pond was overcrowded.

Last time we saw them, these fish had achieved new numbers hovering around the three hundred mark. The largest koi now measure almost forty centimetres, the gold-fish, twenty-five. Obviously, their watery home is of a size and has the resources to suit them all.

Most ponds have an ample supply of natural fish food — aquatic plants, insect larvae and tadpoles. Still, we wanted to have some kind of active relationship with the new arrivals, and decided on a daily feeding. Not excessive — just enough to identify ourselves. We had been told at the fish farm that lettuce and bread-crumbs — wholewheat, cracked wheat or rye — were good for koi in the springtime, after a winter spent in relative lethargy at the bottom of the pond. Otherwise, a special fish food that included carotene, a colour enhancer, would suffice for both koi and goldfish. As for "calling" the fish to feed, almost any signal would do, so long as it was consistent.

There are wooden steps leading down to the water in front of the gazebo. So it is here, every evening, that we bang three times with a stone — and the fish appear. This is not unlike magic — and children are entranced by it. Once, though, the feeding had a rather shocking pay-off, just when I was about to show the fish to visitors.

I went to the steps with the food container, banged the required three times with the stone, and there was the expected surge of movement beneath the surface. A dozen fish — and then a dozen more — rose up and began the usual feeding frenzy.

Well — it might have been the usual feeding frenzy, but it was not the usual fish. Along with the koi and the goldfish, there were others. Small and dark and obviously very young. Who the hell were they? Where had they come from? The pond is land-locked, with the only flow of water coming from the fields in spring, when the thaw is in full flood.

Bill suggested two possible answers. Fish eggs may have arrived from the nearby Beaver River — either on the feet of one of our visiting herons, or clinging to the water lilies we had transplanted to the pond. Or — during the spring flood, it is just possible that small fish from the river may have fought their way upstream. They would have to be extremely small to get through the screening the keeps our fish from escaping through the overflow. But . . . who knows?

By June of its second season, we had asked Len Collins to design and build a Victorian gazebo to be placed among the pond's bordering willows. He made a wonder. It has an oriental cast, as so many Victorian and Edwardian garden structures did, and has become the site of our summer evening ritual. Alone or with friends, and always with wine glass in hand, we sit there in silence, looking out over the water as the sun goes down. As the birds retreat from the sky and the frogs and crickets begin to sing, the moon and stars begin to rise. It is all one could ask for: peace.

Give the gift of water. Give the gift of life. Our pond *is* a gift. To us — and from us. I look at it now and I wonder how I ever doubted its existence. Everyone who sees it says: *it looks as if it has always been there.*

And yes — it does.

And yes — it has been. *If you dig it, it will come.* But only if you dream it first.

A Cavalcade of Friends

*F*OR MORE THAN THREE DECADES THERE HAS BEEN A *welcome stream of visitors to Stone Orchard — old friends and new friends, who have travelled great distances to reach us, or have simply walked down the road. Also our employees over time and once in a while, total strangers. Like Stone Orchard itself, each of them has earned a lasting place in memory.*

The Bucket Brigade

It was a hot, dry August day in 1971 when a grass fire started sweeping across the apple orchard west of the house.

David Lumley, then our teenage helper, had decided to burn a pile of debris built up as a result of his summer's weeding. But Dave hadn't reckoned on the stiff breeze that suddenly sprang up, and soon the fire was threatening the split-rail fence that separated the orchard field from the lawn.

Fortunately, Bill and I were both in the kitchen when Dave came running in to ask for help. We were also lucky to have available more help than usual. Three little girls had walked out from town to visit our twenty-some cats, and to play on the swing in the front yard: Chrissie Warlow, daughter of friends in the village — Margie Butterworth, whose brother, Chuck, had worked for us — and their friend Margie Beddows.

Our water supply was limited in those days — no garden hoses, and not much tap water in the house, since the cistern was almost empty. And so we had to depend on the rain barrels and the hand-pumped well in the back shed.

Thank heaven we had an ample supply of pots and pails. While Dave and Bill ran out to the fire with water-soaked burlap bags to beat out some of the flames, I quickly organized the youngsters into a bucket brigade. I manned the pump while two of them lugged the filled containers out to the fire. The third took on the rain barrels, almost emptying them of their contents.

In fifteen minutes we had brought the runaway fire under control, and by then, all six of us were pouring with perspiration. Bill and I mixed up some lemonade and we gathered around the picnic table to cool off under the trees. It occurred to me that the girls — whom we had dubbed *The Stone Orchard Fire Brigade* — deserved something more than a glass or two of lemonade as a reward for their fire-fighting work, and so I got my change purse and counted out six quarters, intending to give each girl what in those days would have represented a week's allowance — fifty cents.

Chrissie Warlow and Margie Beddows quickly pocketed their loot, but little Margie Butterworth put her hands behind her back and announced in righteous tones: "my mother told me never to accept money from strangers."

Chrissie was disgusted — as only a ten-year-old can be. "Oh, for chrissakes, Margie — take the money!"

She did.

And very shortly afterwards, we upgraded our fire-fighting systems.

It's impossible to live in a rural community and not be aware of the impact of fire on the history of the area. Time after time, we've heard of churches, schools and stores about which we were told: *of course, this isn't the original building. The first one — made of wood — was burned to the ground.*

Bill is even more fire-conscious than I am. When he was a teenager in Regina, he managed to set fire to his grandparents' house.

In case this gives the impression that I've spent several decades living with a pyromaniac, let me assure you: the Regina fire was an accident.

Bill's grandparents had converted the top floor of their house into the ideal retreat for a high-school student — spacious, pleasant and private. This was where Bill took up residence during the school year. In the fall of '48, however, his privacy was briefly interrupted. The living-room furniture was getting new slip-covers and the seamstress was using an old oak library table in Bill's room on which to iron them. One day, when he hurried home to pick up that afternoon's textbooks — and the seamstress was off having lunch — he noticed that she had unplugged his radio/record player to accommodate the use of her iron. This was too much. Bill plugged his record player back in, grabbed his books and dashed off to class. The problem was — by mistake, he had plugged in the iron.

The seamstress had left it — properly unplugged and harmless — sitting flat on the sheets with which she had covered the table. As the iron grew hotter, it not only burned its way through the table, it burned its way through the floor. It then set fire to the wood shavings with which the attic was insulated — and soon, the entire top of the house was ablaze.

Bill was playing tennis after school that afternoon when he got the message: *you'd best come home; the house has burned down.*

Not quite all the way down, but far enough. And the damage was extensive. Although the flames had been confined to the top storey, the fire brigade's hoses had pretty well destroyed all the plaster and hardwood of the lower floors.

Bill and his family moved into a hotel — the carpenters, plumbers and electricians got to work — and Bill developed a healthy habit of never plugging *anything* in without making sure he had the right cord.

The day of Dave Lumley's grass fire was as close as we ever came, at Stone Orchard, to needing what had grown out of our community's original bucket brigade — the band of intrepid volunteer firefighters who work out of the Cannington Station.

Things have changed a lot since the days when the men were called to action by the ringing of the old firebell. For years, Gertie Graham had done the ringing, living as she did only a couple of doors away from the hall. For almost three decades, her husband Hank was Chief — just as his father, Thomas, had been before him. People used to say they could tell how big a fire it was by the urgency of Gertie's ringing.

Sadly, both Gert and Hank are gone now, and as of this year so is their son, Gary. He had been Chief for the past eight years — with altogether thirty-three years of service as a firefighter. With Gary's son and nephew among the twenty-two men in the brigade, we still think of it as a family affair.

Eventually, the bell gave way to a siren, and under the new system the men respond to electronic calls. Seven of them carry radios while the rest have pagers. Their heavy equipment includes two pumpers, a tanker, a rescue truck and — thanks to local service clubs — a heavy-duty extricator with huge steel pincers and clippers. They call it the *Jaws of Life,* and it can rescue people trapped in wrecked cars. The men are trained to deal with fires, accidents and medical emergencies — the latter making up almost forty percent of their calls.

The first time we saw them in action it was on a night in the late sixties, when the sound of the siren was followed by a rush of traffic past our house. Looking out the window we saw that the whole sky to the west was lit up. Fearing a fire right next door, at the Purvises, we got into the car and headed down the road — wanting to help, if we could. To our amazement, we had to drive almost three miles before we reached the site of the fire — a burning barn.

I can never forget — though I wish I could — what I saw there, and heard. The blaze was already uncontrollable by the time it had been discovered. What is worse, the terrified cattle had retreated into the farthest reaches of the burning building — and there was no way to get them out. It was a night of tragedy and horror. Even now, as I write these words, I can see and hear again the flames and cries and feel the same utter helplessness that held us all at bay.

Today, with improvements in fire prevention and detection, in water supply and communication, such tragedies are becoming rare.

Bless everyone — and everything — that keep them so.

Road Show

The kitchen window at Stone Orchard looks out at the 11th Concession of Brock Township. The view is framed by a wide proscenium arch of front-yard trees, creating a stage upon which a year-long, wondrous road show is played. If you go beyond the gate and look west, you seem to be facing a painted backdrop for a pastoral piece of Victorian theatre. Or perhaps a dramatic reading of "The Highwayman." The road's perspective is perfectly drawn, its rolling contours leading the eye to a vanishing point beyond which all the world — both past and present — can be imagined. And gained.

On such a road, not far from here, the boy who grew up to be my grandfather rode the post horse, learning how to read with book in hand, as he delivered mail in the 1870s. On another road nearby, Bill's great-grandfather stood outside his inn at Vallentyne, handing over the list of his 1861 assets to the census-taker: *one cow, two pigs and a barrel of whisky . . .*

I once watched Bill himself come over the crest of that vanishing point, a figure seemingly striding through the dust from another time. The car had died on the highway, and Bill was weighted down with two suitcases, his coat, like an actor's cape, thrown over his shoulder. This image gave new meaning to the phrase *strolling player.*

One of the most memorable features of the passing parade belongs to the time just shortly after we had moved into Stone Orchard. I was on my knees doing some weeding in the front yard when I heard the approach of a rumbling, rattling vehicle coming up the hill from the river. I saw it was Leonard Griffin, driving his team as they pulled the manure spreader. The horses were jingling with all the accoutrements of equine harnessing and decoration; the spreader — an old one — was banging its metal wheels along the washboard surface of the road — and Leonard was singing out a steady stream of hymns.

Having just pulled out another dandelion, I was sitting back on my heels to watch the whole rig as it started to come abreast of me. At that point, Leonard spotted me and, being neighbourly, decided it was only polite to stop and offer me a "good day." This meant many *hup*s and *haw*s and *whoa*s before the whole contraption rocked to a halt.

Leonard's "good day" wasn't quite what I expected. As he took off his hat and wiped his brow with his sleeve — and as the horses stood, clomping their hooves and snorting, Leonard looked at me and said: *you know, Tim, I can't help remarking . . . how short life is . . .*

With that — and many more *ho*s and *hup*s — Leonard and his helpers started up again and proceeded along the road — leaving me hunkered there, my dead, uprooted dandelion dangling from my hand.

It was enchanting.

There was a child — an eight-year-old girl — we found once on the road. This was not enchanting. She was walking to school, mid-winter — grim-faced and pale, with tears drying on her cheeks. She wore a buttonless summer coat, a cotton dress two sizes too large and a pair of running shoes with no laces. Once we had driven her to the school and spoken to her teacher, we telephoned the appropriate authorities, only to be told that nothing could be done *because both her parents are at home and she has not been abandoned.* In my opinion, she had been entirely abandoned, but that was not the reading given by the authorities. Still, that was some time ago. The girl survived and, I trust, has long since abandoned her parents.

Over time we have seen a good many characters walk across this stage. Mister Irwin, known as *The Professor*, who took up residence in the retired schoolhouse at the corner after he himself had retired as a teacher. Black coat — black hat — black cotton gloves. And a black leather bag, not unlike the cases carried once by doctors. Nobody knew what was in the bag. Surgical instruments? Five million dollars? The head of a murder victim? Certainly, he was odd. And magical. The gentlest man in all the world, if you took him as he was — slightly unbalanced due to what he called a brain fever — a man who talked to the wind and carried nothing more alarming in his bag than laundry, a pair of rubbers for rainy weather and a change purse from which he counted pennies. Once a month or so, he would arrive at lunchtime, plodding into the yard as if he'd walked ten thousand miles — and accept a glass of milk, two fried-egg sandwiches and a cup of tea. Afterwards, he would depart, never having removed his overcoat because it was safety-pinned instead of buttoned — and all the cats would trail off after him down the road like a string of converts following a saint.

Sometimes in winter, the road show offers figures that might have stepped from *Doctor Zhivago* — scarved and mittened, woollen-hatted — round, blue figures encased in down or Mackinaw jackets, walking through blizzards, windblown and nearly blinded by snow. These are the *health-nuts,* who in summer speed by in shorts and running shoes with red bandanna head-scarves and Walkman ear-plugs. Children also pass, calling out the names of lost dogs and cats. Riders in tan coats and black hats, cyclists in yellow Lycra, women in cotton dresses, walking arm in arm and shielded from the sun with green umbrellas. It gets quite colourful out there.

On rare occasions, praise be, someone will drive past pointing out the blue house and the stone wall for visitors who stare without apology and nod their heads. *Celebrities, you say. Well!* The car will then return, moving more slowly than before, so the visitors on the other side can be told about the famous and their cats. *And what might they be doing in there today?*

Hiding.

Cars have actually parked out front and once — thank heaven, only once — a woman left the driver's seat, got out and flourished her binoculars, staring at us from the road.

A boy was killed by the gates, in a head-on collision. His brothers had made a bet that he couldn't drive to the liquor store before it closed and be home again within ten minutes. The speedometer in his wrecked car had locked at 80 m.p.h. Happily, those in the other vehicle — a truck — survived.

There is a hill just in front of us, and a plethora of demon drivers. Many dead or injured cats — many dead or injured dogs. Multiple road-kills. And a boy on a bike in the dark — one recent night — hit by a speeding truck. Pelvis broken — arm broken — face battered — leg nearly severed. Therapy first, then amputation and an artificial limb.

Well, these things happen, someone said.

Yes, but only when drivers don't give a damn.

One last image — a tribute to a departed friend. This was Arthur Boissonneau, whose wife, Alice, is also a writer and an old acquaintance of mine. Before retirement, Arthur had been a government naturalist — a kind of census-taker in the world of plants. All the last years of his life, he went with his water spaniel to the ditches of our road — and others — collecting edible pods and berries, wild asparagus, pausing to note the activities of birds and insects. Animals. His presence was a signal that all was well. How could the world be at odds with a man whose passion for its wonders led him through its ditches? He died one April, making his garden. His dog was with him. Alice, making lunch, was singing in the kitchen. Sad as it was, it was fitting. But I couldn't help but think of Leonard Griffin and *how short life is* . . . The view from our window of the passing road show will not be the same without Arthur Boissonneau.

Or, for that matter, without Leonard Griffin, who died some years ago.

Hail and farewell — to both.

The Kitchen Stove

For a while our only source of heat at Stone Orchard was the wood stove in the kitchen. Its pipes snaked through the living-room and the upstairs bedrooms before reaching the chimney on the roof. They offered heat to parts of the house — but not enough for writers sitting at their desks. And as winter approached — our first in the house — we were glad we hadn't put all our money into the down payment. We had deliberately saved an even thousand dollars for whatever might be essential to the new home — and so we installed an oil furnace, and simplified the course of the stovepipe.

We kept the wood stove, however, and for years it served all our cooking needs — in the kitchen in the winter, and out back in the pantry during the summer. Its reservoir ensured a constant supply of hot water, even when storms produced lengthy cuts in our electricity, which would hit both our new pressure pump and water heater. Its oven gave the best possible crust to every loaf of bread — and there has never been anything like the even heat it lent to the frying pan for bacon and perfect eggs. "Awesome eggs," as one of our teenage helpers dubbed them — Saturday chores are always, in our house, sweetened by the prospect of arriving to a full, home-cooked breakfast.

The old stove, however, was not without its hazards. During one of the first visits made to Stone Orchard by Bill's parents, we had to spend a day in Toronto. When we got home, we found the parents tight-lipped, shaking — and packed, ready to leave. Nothing we could find to say would persuade them to stay.

Finally, they told us what had happened. In our absence, they had decided to do us the favour of a kitchen clean-up. Scour the sink, scrub the countertops — burn the garbage.

Burn the garbage. Ah, yes . . . To this day, we don't know how it happened, but somewhere in the garbage, there had been a can of peas. An unopened can. Into the stove it went, along with the burnables. And out of the stove it came — explosively. The stove lids hit the ceiling — along with what was described as about a ton of soot and ashes. It had taken all day to clean up the mess. All day, except the time it took to pack.

Yes, they left the next morning — but after that, their visits were longer — and far more pleasant.

We had our first electric stove on one of those later visits, when Bill's mother taught us a delicious dessert — particularly useful for unexpected company. It was called, simply, *Crunch*:

Into a buttered, ovenproof baking dish (about 10 inches square and 2^{1}/$_{2}$ inches deep) pour a can of cherry pie filling and spread it around. Sprinkle a single white cake mix over this, and top with a further sprinkling of about ^{2}/$_{3}$ cup of sliced almonds. Dribble ^{2}/$_{3}$ cup of melted butter over all, and bake at 350°F for about 45 minutes. Serve warm with a topping of whipped cream or ice cream. Youngsters are crazy for it. Oldsters go mad. *Midsters*, as we were then, sit back and pray the guests don't eat it all. By the way, you can also make it with peach or apple, blueberry or apricot filling — but the best of all is cherry.

My own mother's contribution to our "emergency recipes" was also a dessert — and just as simple, just as delicious. *Mocha Mousse:*

> In a double boiler, dissolve 24 marshmallows in 1 cup of hot, strong coffee, stirring frequently. Let the mixture cool, and refrigerate until it begins to thicken. Then fold in 1 cup of cream, whipped, and 1 tsp. vanilla. Place into a serving dish and sprinkle the top with 1 grated square of unsweetened chocolate. Chill and serve. And stand back. The stampede may *getcha!*

There were often times in summer, of course, when neither heat nor hot food could be tolerated — and then, whatever stove it was, we gave it a rest.

This was the time for one of Beverley Roberts's cold soups. Beverley is an old friend from Bill's Saskatoon days. Her gift of the following ultra-simple recipe has remained one of our mainstays, no matter where we are.

Mix equal quantities of cold buttermilk and cold vegetable juice — tomato, clamato or garden cocktail are best. Season with salt and pepper, a squeeze of lemon and a touch of Worcestershire sauce. Pour into a tureen and garnish with fresh herbs (basil seems to work for most juices). Serve with a flourish, pretending — if you like — that it's taken hours to prepare.

Our last stove at Stone Orchard was definitely — and literally — of industrial strength. This was a gas range designed for restaurant use — with a large griddle and a gas broiler called a salamander. The griddle was ideal for feeding breakfast to a houseful of guests — bacon and eggs, pancakes and sausage, homefries . . . And the salamander did perfect steaks as well as such incredible desserts as *crème brûlée*. Bill always uses the Alice B. Toklas recipe for the latter, which is basically a custard of egg yolks and cream, slowly cooked and chilled until set and then covered with a centimetre or two of sifted brown sugar. Careful broiling produces a sweet, crunchy top that has to be cracked with the back of a spoon before the dessert can be served. Alice knew a thing or two when it came to food. This is a classic.

The griddle was also used for a Stone Orchard specialty, Pork Picatta. I no longer eat veal, and so Bill adapted this heavenly Italian dish to either pork or chicken:

> Cut a pork tenderloin into 1-inch slices. Pound each slice thinly. Bill does this by placing the meat between two empty freezer bags, and pounding it with a wooden mallet. Dredge with seasoned flour and fry in batches — depending on the size of your skillet — about one minute per side, using a very hot mixture of olive oil and butter. When all the meat is cooked and set aside in a covered dish, add a bit more butter to the pan, and enough leftover dredging flour to produce a *roux*. Deglaze the pan with enough white wine and half as much lemon juice to produce the desired amount of sauce. Cook until slightly thickened, season with salt, pepper and fresh chopped parsley. Reheat the meat in the sauce and serve.

We offer this with basmati rice plus a mountain of zucchini and red pepper strips, sautéed quickly and lightly in olive oil — with or without a touch of garlic.

Over the years, we have settled on a standard menu for larger dinner parties: a whole tenderloin of beef, brushed with a mixture of melted butter and Kitchen Bouquet seasoning and roasted for about 45 minutes at 500°F. This produces a roast both rare and medium rare. In Cannington, we have been extremely lucky to have Ron Butterworth as our butcher. His pork and beef are exemplary — the beef among the best we've ever had. We serve it accompanied by sliced potatoes cooked (oven or microwave) in olive oil with a *lot* of garlic. The green vegetable is usually a blend of two purées: spinach and parsnip, seasoned with lots of butter, salt, pepper and a bit of nutmeg.

One of our most memorable dinners was served on Canada Day, July 1, 1985. When we were about to set the table, we discovered that with house guests and other visitors — including our current teenage helper, Barry Spence and his entire family — there would be thirteen at table. This made everyone uneasy until we remembered we had the perfect additional guest for that particular day. He usually sat in my bedroom in the form of a stunning ventriloquist's doll — a memento from a play I had written for Bill Hutt, who played the title role: John A. Macdonald. And so, we set that extra place and enjoyed our celebratory beef in the company of our first prime minister.

The Hockey Net

A few years ago, Speaker Nicholson died. No one was prepared to hear of it. It seemed impossible. He was only sixty. And I guess we all thought Jessie, his mother, wouldn't allow it to happen.

Jessie was then in her eighties. If life were a hockey game and death were the referee, Jessie would have told him to go to hell — and given him a thwack with her purse. She's been known to do this at the local arena whenever she hears a bad call.

In some ways, life itself was a hockey game to Jessie Nicholson. Her sons and grandsons and now her great-grandsons have all put on skates and headed for centre ice. This all began when her daughter, Toots, married Garnet MacLeish. Garnet loved hockey with a passion. You can't be a hockey fan and not know who Rick MacLeish is. Ex-star of the Philadelphia Flyers. Well, he's Garnet's son and Jessie's grandson.

When Speaker died, almost twelve hundred people filed two abreast into the visitation at the local funeral parlour. This from a community of only eighteen hundred. It was breath-taking. The line stretched all the way down Laidlaw Street to the other side of the Beaver River bridge — almost two blocks.

Two silent policemen in dress uniform stood by the doors. The Volunteer Fire Brigades of Cannington and two neighbouring villages also attended in uniform — the men in blue and the Ladies' Auxiliaries in fiery red blazers. Speaker's fellow truckers were also there. And every amateur hockey player from miles around, flowing in through the doors with their families — but none with an explanation of Speaker's nickname. Few even knew he'd been christened Ronald.

In time we heard the family legend, which told that Ronald Nicholson came into the world with a roar. Not quite *he shoots — he scores!* — but the next best thing. When his parents suggested that a little quiet might be a blessing, their son went right on talking. This way he got his name. If one who speaks is a speaker, then *Speaker* it would be. He never shed it. It stayed with him for life.

His funeral saw *the hockey net* in action — the net that had been spun by its matriarch. They had all come out for Speaker, for his wife, Grace, and his children — and for his mother, Jessie. Bill and I long ago became happily enmeshed in the hockey net. This was in the sixties, when Speaker's nephew Donnie started carrying our groceries out to the car from the local supermarket. Now, Donnie's wife, Jo Ann, works at the bank, dispensing dollars and sense and one of the warmest smiles in Cannington. Michael, their son, joined the ongoing ranks of Nicholsons and MacLeishes who have worked, over time, at Stone Orchard.

Some memories of these younger members of the clan are best told without using names; we value our lives.

One of them involves the first and only time that any of the teenagers took an active interest in gardening. Specifically, in the greenhouse. For a while, it was the first place they visited after arriving for work. Eventually, to our amusement, we discovered why. Our winter geraniums were found to be sheltering a small crop of what might be termed "a smokeable substance." The boys finally agreed to abandon their "garden" when we pointed out the dangers of such a crop — not to them, but to us, a pair of reasonably respectable writers — if it was ever found on our property.

Then there was the lad who spent hours, at home, talking to his girlfriend on the phone. A younger member of his family used to listen in. She was seven, and one day asked their mother the meaning of an expression the girlfriend had fondly used. "What's a *stud muffin*, Mother?" Mother, somewhat taken aback, immediately wanted to know where it had been heard. The explanation was both honest and complete. *Aha*! And the next time the young Lothario called home to say that a hockey practice would make him late for supper, Mother replied: "that's fine. And thanks for phoning . . . *Stud Muffin*!"

Speaker's son Brad was the first of our Nicholson/MacLeish helpers. Later, we proudly watched him skate his way to a hockey scholarship in the States, where he took a business degree. That was when we learned that hockey players can be just as tough and determined off the ice as on. For a solid year, while he worked slinging crates of Coke from the back of a truck, Brad tried to find a job that would give him scope to apply his education. He would come out to the farm every week or so, and ask to use the computer. Heaven knows how many résumés he mailed or how many job applications he filed. A lot, that's for certain, and non-stop.

Finally — and hallelujah — his persistence paid off. Not only with a job, but — shortly after — a marriage and now a family.

When Brad and his wife, Kim, brought their firstborn, Brooke, on visits, we decided that given her lineage, we might soon be hearing the cry: *she shoots! — she scores!*

Brad's sister Trish used to scold us whenever work pressure drove us back to the drugstore to ask her for cigarettes. Now, of course, the drugstore no longer sells cigarettes, but Trish is still there with an admonishing look in her eye. Sherrin, another sister, comes to the farm on a regular basis to cut our hair. Her electric energy drives her tongue as fast as it drives her scissors — but only the scissors have a cutting edge. Our tonsorial evenings always end with a glass of wine, a meal — and laughter.

There is a special treat if Sherrin cooks the meal; by popular demand, in our house, it is her angel hair spaghetti, prepared as suggested by another Cannington friend, Peho Marshak. It involves an hour's cooking of tomatoes and sliced pimento olives with garlic and olive oil, salt and pepper. Meanwhile, grate Mozzarella cheese (about 500 grams to serve three or four) and ultimately, cook the angel hair. Turn the drained spaghetti into a bowl, then the cheese, and then the steaming hot tomato and olive mixture. Covering the bowl for a few minutes lets the sauce melt the cheese. Toss and serve with a salad. Terrific!

The MacLeish side of the clan entered our lives when Tom, another of Jessie's grandsons, married Julie Collins, Len's sister. Scott, their eldest, was among our last employees. One fall day he arrived sporting a bizarre haircut given to all the rookies who made it onto the local team. "Yes?" we said, expecting an explanation. "Oh, it's nothing," he told us. "Just a haircut." Scott and his working buddy, Mike Norris — another hockey star — tried to turn the pond into a rink one winter, but their efforts were thwarted by record snow falls and killer winds. In the summer, they used to hang an old tire from a tree beside the pond, and, during their breaks, take turns being Tarzan — swinging out over the water and dropping down like cannonballs. This no doubt gave the koi heart attacks, but the fish had their revenge by trying to make a meal of human toes.

Tom and Julie's youngest son is named Jesse — partly in honour of his great-grandmother. Like most of the boys in the clan, he was made to walk around the house at the age of two — wearing skates. *It strengthens the ankles and develops balance.* At age two and a half, Jesse won the prize as youngest on the ice at a local skating event. The eldest — of course — was his great-grandmother.

We were away when Jessie died. Sherrin made sure we knew, however, and from a distance we joined the whole community in tribute to one of our most remarkable citizens. And even now, stories of Jessie's life we hadn't heard before keep surfacing.

Some time ago, she began to wonder why it was that her splendid Victorian house had taken up singing to her on summer afternoons. *A low, sweet humming sound,* she said, *like a distant choir* . . . But there had never been an explanation. Then, one day her family arrived to replace the old siding and there it was. A hive, from top to bottom, of golden honeycomb.

Bill and I had to smile, when we heard about it. *Honeycomb.* And why not — for the matriarch of our hockey net — the Queen Bee of hockey.

Absent Friends

Our memories are furnished with indelible images of the many people who have, over the years, been part of our lives at Cannington. When it came time to pack up belongings and move them out of Stone Orchard, where we had made our home for more than half our lives, we discovered just how many mementos we had of our friends, many of whom — too many — are now dead.

Setting out our favourite red goblets for safe packing — along with a red glass punch bowl, we remembered Marg and Jack Treweek, who had given us these as house-warming gifts. Marg had once been a secretary in the offices of the CBC radio program "The Learning Stage" — which later became known as "Ideas." It was that program that paid us the money with which to start buying Stone Orchard. We slaved there — and happily — for five years.

Marg was the epitome of British effervescence. Her bubbling coloratura laugh — she was something of a singer — and her endless enthusiasm made a lovely contrast to Jack's quieter charms. I particularly remember one summer walk in the lower meadow and woodlot. Marg suddenly spotted a garter snake sunning itself on a rock. It is sufficient to say that she was not fond of reptiles. Her soprano scream — almost an aria — pierced the air all the way back up the hill and over the fields to the house. Our handyman, then, was Doug Bursey. Working on a window frame, he stopped, listened and decided the neighbours must be playing their favourite opera a bit too loud. As for the snake — he fled and doubtless took up a more peaceful life elsewhere.

The first Treweek son, Laurence, was Bill's godchild, although, when the second one arrived — James — we treated them both as part of our family. By then, the Treweeks had gone back to Britain and were living in a tiny house, somehow managing to give both boys the education they wanted. Laurence is now a successful computer animator working in California for the likes of Steven Spielberg, while James is carving out a place in the London music world as a successful jazz pianist.

And Marg and Jack? A recent phone call from James provided the numbing news that both his parents had suffered instantaneous death when a tractor-trailer went out of control and ran head-on into their car.

We got out the red glasses, filled them with wine and offered the same toast that has been drunk at every Stone Orchard dinner party we can remember: *to absent friends.*

One of my oldest and closest friends died in 1990, during one of the hardest weeks I have ever endured. In that short period, other deaths included my aged mother; my favourite cat; our oldest dog; the mother of a close friend and another friend who chose suicide. That oldest, closest friend was Janet Baldwin, whom I had known since I was six or seven and she was eighteen. She had been my dance teacher before we discovered that a vertebral problem would not allow me to become the dancer I wanted to be — and so I shifted my focus, first, to the life of an actor, and finally, a writer. Janet, being older, was in between my parents' generation and my own, and yet her manner remained to the end that of a wonderfully innocent child. Eyes wide open with delight and interest; a smile that seemed to take over her whole face; a high, shy, always questioning voice. But nobody who really knew Janet was fooled. Her manner and its impetus were real — but behind them lay a dedicated artist and a shrewd business woman. Following an unhappy divorce, she had run her own ballet school for years and made a great success of it.

What we have now of Janet — apart from our bonded memories of how much she loved and depended on the haven of Stone Orchard — is her likeness. She is portrayed in a terracotta bust, created by sculptor Patricia Brennan as part of her *Angels and Archangels* series. These magical figures show a roomful of artists from Toronto's dance world. The dancers are presented as angels, complete with wings — and include Rudolf Nureyev and Erik Brühn, plus others who have died. The men and women who played important roles in the world of teaching or the birth of Canada's National Ballet are seen as larger busts. The whole effect is stunning.

It was through Janet that we met the artist Bill Bryan — a former dancer and pupil of Janet's who was also a talented, self-taught painter. Over time, the walls of Stone Orchard came to display more and more of Bill's work: a portrait of my mother, clothed in a blue tweed coat for which Bill Whitehead had woven the material; a study of the "milking tree," whose spreading arms eventually succumbed to Dutch elm disease; three simple sketches drawn in blue crayon and displayed in antique oval frames; and a brilliant series of "yellow-on-yellow" paintings — one, of the field across the road, the others, still lifes.

Bill Bryan and I shared a birthday. The last one we shared was just before Janet Baldwin's death in 1990; Bill himself died shortly afterwards.

We later learned that we had been driving past the hospital where Janet lay dying, as we were on our way to say a final goodbye to another friend — Rob Read. We were about to leave on an extended book tour, and we knew that AIDS would claim Rob's life before we returned.

Rob — who incidentally had also been a dancer — and his companion, the writer Alberto Manguel, were traditional New Year's guests at Stone Orchard. Every New Year's Eve we played a video murder mystery game — one that was supposed to come with a sheet of red plastic that had to be used in order to read some of the game's secret information. When Rob and Albee arrived with the game in its box, they had forgotten that essential piece of plastic. Fortunately, we had been given a large glass plate intended for serving sandwiches in Edwardian times — and it was red. Most of the year we kept it on display, but on December 31st, we brought it down to help us solve our murder mysteries. It served very well, but since Rob's death, it has been retired to its place on display.

Since the early 1980s it has been sadly impossible to work in the arts without losing many friends to AIDS. Not that AIDS has not struck outside the arts community, but in our own early experience of this plague, it took a mighty toll amongst homosexual theatre, writing and painting companions. Later, it widened its range of targets and the results have been devastating.

In response to those untimely deaths, when Toronto's Casey House opened in 1987 to become Canada's leading AIDS hospice, Bill and I joined the dozens of others who volunteered to work there. For two and a half years, we travelled to Toronto once a week to spend the day at the hospice. Bill, who hates the telephone, nonetheless loved his job as switchboard operator and receptionist — while I worked mostly on the residents' floor, doing whatever I could to alleviate pressures on the nursing staff — such mundane jobs as running baths and making tea. It was also my responsibility to organize a series of entertainments, which included readings by some of Canada's best known writers — each of whom came to Casey House and sat downstairs in a charmed circle of rapt listeners. Everyone came who was asked: Jane Rule, Michael Ondaatje, Alice Munro, Linda Griffiths, Pierre Berton, Alberto Manguel, June Callwood, Margaret Atwood — plus the American novelist John Irving. At Christmastime a concert was given with pianist Stuart Hamilton and singers Maureen Forrester and Rose Marie Landry. The memory of these events is indelible.

But what does all this have to do with Stone Orchard? A lot. Each summer, we hosted days in the country for everyone at Casey House who was able to travel — residents, nurses, staff and Board members. Such days were spent largely around the swimming pool, with plenty of drink and an array of Bill's popular cooking.

Those were special times for both of us, since we became friends with so many Casey House people. June Callwood, the miraculous moving force behind the creation of the hospice, was already an old friend — and was soon joined by dozens of others whose lives had been touched, affected and changed forever by AIDS. Our great affection for the nursing staff was augmented by a sense of awe and wonder at their dedication, courage and compassion. Their boundless devotion to those in their care was not only inspiring, it was shaming. Whenever I think I'm tired, I realize I don't know the half of it. Our fellow volunteers were a glorious mixed bag of genders and generosities, coming from every walk of life, every age group and every interest. The residents themselves unwittingly taught us more than anyone we have ever known about the grace of living — and the courage of dying.

A few of these wonderful men came to spend private times at Stone Orchard — sometimes alone or with special companions. One of these was a young man named Dan, a gentle smiling redhead who totally captured our hearts. Two of his passions were swimming pools and stiff martinis. Luckily, we could — and did — provide both. When Dan shyly admitted he was an artist and showed us some of his paintings, we immediately asked to buy two of them.

Wherever we are — wherever we look — we will see these portraits, landscapes, still lifes and photographs of Casey House summer afternoons — along with the other mementos of unforgotten love — sculptures, red glass plates and goblets. And still we raise our glasses in salute to all our absent friends — including, now, Stone Orchard itself.

From Stone Orchard

*S*EASONS CHANGE, THE YEARS PASS, PEOPLE AGE. *The time has come for us to leave the farm. Our work continues — so do our lives, with our time divided between France and Stratford, Ontario. In memory, however, we will always remain at home in Stone Orchard.*

Across the road, the field through which I sometimes walk on my way to town rolls up gently to a crest, sliding away on the other side towards the old railroad bed and the Beaver River. Mornings and evenings, I sit at the kitchen window and watch Len Collins's cattle grazing there with their calves. When they stand against the skyline at dusk, they create a pastoral image that, for me, tells why we live where we do. *Here* would not be *here* without that field.

Most of one recent summer, however, Bill and I were not watching cattle — we were watching goats. They were browsing on scrub brush in an abandoned olive grove beside a vineyard. Clearly, we were not at Stone Orchard.

We were in France — on the outskirts of the Provençal village of Cotignac — having gone there in order to escape the phone and the FAX while a book got finished. Evenings, we sat looking down the terraced hillside at the scene below us. The *chevrier* was the classic goatherd: carrying a crook, wearing a wide, white hat, with a wineskin slung on his back. His constant companions — aside from the bearded flock — were a tanned young woman and a lame black dog. This, then, became the pastoral image of where we were. *There* would not have been *there* without it.

Two small communities, two unique countrysides — each in its way a stand-in for paradise. But paradise tempered with a healthy dose of reality. In Provence, there is often merciless heat and drought — in southern Ontario, merciless cold and damp. The essence of both these places lies in the word *survival*.

Being in Cotignac gave me distance enough and perspective with which to view my home community, and a deeper appreciation of what it offers — and what it demands in terms of survival. The trip abroad also revealed surprising parallels between these two distinctive places, and confirmed our decision, thirty years ago, to put down roots in a rural setting.

Across the road, I watched a calf being born one spring. Then I saw all the other members of the herd — including Len's pony, Dolly — approach the newborn and give it a good nosing. Finally, I watched the cow eating most of the after-birth — sensing instinctively what to do, without, as far as I can tell, knowing that the hormones it contained would stimulate the flow of the right kind of milk for her offspring. As she urged the calf to its feet and guided it to her udder, some crows flew down from the trees and finished what remained of the afterbirth. In half an hour there was not a trace of evidence — no telltale signs for predators. Nature's efficiency more often than not can take your breath away.

At Cotignac, one evening, we watched a kid being born in the abandoned vineyard below our house. This was a difficult birth, accompanied by a fair amount of vocalization from the nanny. The goatherd knew what to do and went to her aid. When he finally stood up, he removed his shirt and wrapped it around the newborn. Clutching the kid to his chest, he led a procession away from the field towards the home pasture. He and the newborn were followed closely by the nanny. Then came the rest of the herd, in single file — and bringing up the rear, the beautiful young woman and the lame black dog. As we watched them disappear from view, we almost expected music — pan pipes, perhaps — and a final curtain descending slowly over the scene. It was pure theatrical magic.

Cannington and Cotignac — each with a population of fewer than two thousand — each with its individual anchor in history — each with its future in question. Their merchants must now compete with the giant malls and supermarkets of neighbouring towns; their surrounding countrysides face the threat — still distant, I'm glad to say — of urban sprawl. Still, the early signs are there in both cases, and it's worrying.

Both communities have their special festivals. Early every winter, Cannington musters local talent and pizazz to mount a Santa Claus parade. This event can be glorious. And hilarious. Over time, Saint Nick's padding swells and thins — as tall men, short men, fat men and skinny men put on the suit. One year, Saint Nick himself rode down Cameron Street. It must have been him, because all the local red-and-whites were still in mothballs. No one every tracked him down, the North Pole being too distant. On another occasion, Nora Joyce, our miracle of a housekeeper, donned the suit and rode the sleigh. The only trace of Nora was her merry eyes. She was the best Saint Nick we've seen.

Late every summer, Cotignac stages a wine festival, during which an enormous papier-mâché Bacchus is paraded round the *cours* — the central square where all the café tables sit under the plane trees. His appearance is preceded by locals in musketeer costume, firing their ancient muskets into the air. All the dogs go mad when the guns go off and they tear around the streets barking up a storm. As Bacchus passes, the whole population is there to cheer him on with a stirring anthem and a raised glass. An exhilarating, heady climax.

On the banks of the Beaver River, which passes through Cannington, there is a park laid out beneath maple trees. Here, the War Memorial stands, and a benevolent fountain offers a wading pool to dogs and children. Picnic tables and tennis courts compete for attention — as does the nearby baseball diamond. Every summer weekend sees a boisterous community or family celebration. And there's a bowling green, with Edwardian echoes of white-clad players and a green-and-white pavilion.

All of this has its counterpart in Cotignac, where the *cours* spreads its welcome beneath its canopy of trees. In their shade, the several cafés, bars and restaurants compete for our attention and, on market day, music is provided by strolling guitarists and singers. Even, time to time, by violinists. Down on the sandy flats beyond the square, old and young alike play at boule — a unique and lovely game to watch, demanding skill and panache. The *thwack* of metal balls punctuates the evening's conversation. Boule is a social game, and the sense of civilized camaraderie is one of its great pleasures.

The War Memorial in Cotignac sits in front of the *mairie* — the town hall. You reach it by climbing up through winding streets, passing old fountains set in tiny, green parks. The water from their stone spouts has flowed all the way from the Alps and is clear and cold and pure. Citizens bring their jugs and fill them there while they gossip. The memorial itself depicts a helmeted infantryman peering from his trench and beneath him, on the marble, are printed the names of *les enfants de Cotignac* — the children of Cotignac — who gave up their lives in both world wars. It is the same at Cannington, and what is saddest in both locations is the repetition of family names — the same, again and again.

Each village, too, has its local volunteer fire brigade. In Cotignac, its members are called *les pompiers* — and, like their Cannington counterparts, they are also on call to help with medical emergencies and road accidents. Survival depends on all these services. There can be no security without them.

If there is a notable difference, it is in the strength of tradition. In France — in the villages, at least, businesses have resisted consolidation. Yes, there are huge supermarkets in the nearby towns — also dotting the autoroutes between the towns — but in the smallest places, you buy your magazines at the *presse* and your cigarettes at the *tabac* and — apart from market day — your vegetables at the *alimentaire,* your meat at the *boucherie,* your bread at the *boulangerie* and your desserts at the *patisserie* . . . etc.

This helps account for the fact that — unlike Cannington — there is hardly any unemployment in Cotignac.

As for the pleasures of the weekly market — and of café tables in the open air — we kept asking ourselves: *why not in Cannington?* Ontario farms grow vegetables; our summers are almost as warm and sunny for outdoor dining. The only answer we've ever found is: *Canada chose something else.* And, as we watch how difficult it is for Cannington, itself, to survive as a community, we wonder if the choice was right. We even wonder if it was conscious, or if it was simply the sum total of a whole series of minor, day-to-day decisions that didn't seem important at the time. As examples of these choices, Cotignac has three bakeries plus the pastry shop; Cannington has none. And while Cotignac has eight cafés and bars, Cannington barely supports two, plus a small pizza palace. Enough said.

Still, the rest of what these two villages share is still present — a strong sense of place — a keen awareness of tradition — a neighbourly society — and a setting of haunting beauty. These are the ongoing legacies of rural life — both there, and here.

As for Cotignac, now that we have bought the house we originally stayed in, we will go back there once or twice every year. It is where the writing now gets done, and so we call it *Mots Maison.* Word House. And we will always return to

Cannington — even if only in our dreams — and to Stone Orchard. We will always live there in our hearts. There is no escaping the pull of home, with its sight of Len's cattle standing on their hill, the cries of the killdeer and the moonlit silence of the pond.